SYSTEMATIC COUNTRY DIAGNOSTICS

From Uneven Growth to Inclusive Development

Romania's Path to Shared Prosperity

WORLD BANK GROUP

Contents

Acknowledgments

This report was written by a team co-led by Donato De Rosa (Lead Economist, World Bank), Yeon Soo Kim (Economist, World Bank), and Aimilios Chatzinikolaou (Senior Operations Officer, International Finance Corporation; IFC), and including David Bulman (Assistant Professor, Johns Hopkins University SAIS), Andrei Silviu Dospinescu (Consultant, World Bank), Jonathan Karver (Research Analyst, World Bank), Craig Meisner (Senior Environmental Economist, World Bank), Maja Murisic (Environmental Specialist, World Bank), Catalin Pauna (Senior Economist, World Bank), and Vincent de Paul Tsoungui Belinga (Economist, World Bank). The team received guidance from Arup Banerji (Country Director, World Bank), Tatiana Proskuryakova (Country Manager, World Bank), Lalita Moorty (Practice Manager, World Bank), Luis-Felipe Lopez-Calva (Practice Manager, World Bank), Thomas Lubeck (Manager, IFC), Gjergj Konda (Principal Economist, IFC), Christian Bodewig (Program Leader, World Bank), Andrea Liverani (Program Leader, World Bank), and Rogier van den Brink (Program Leader, World Bank). The team is thankful to peer reviewers Ulrich Bartsch (Lead Economist, World Bank), Pedro Rodriguez (Program Leader, World Bank), and Carlos Rodriguez Castelan (Senior Economist, World Bank) for their comments.

Many staff contributed to this report, with inputs to specific chapters and to the preparation of a series of background notes that helped inform this diagnostic. The main contributors are listed below.

GLOBAL PRACTICE OR GLOBAL THEME	TEAM MEMBER(S)
Agriculture	Edinaldo Tebaldi, Hans Christoph Kordik
Education	Mariana Doina Moarcas, Alina Sava, Janssen Edelweiss, Nunes Teixeira
Energy and Extractives	Rome Chavapricha, Dejan Ostojic, Paivi Koljonen
Environment and Natural Resources	Craig Meisner, Maja Murisic, Cesar Niculescu

(continued)

GLOBAL PRACTICE OR GLOBAL THEME	TEAM MEMBER(S)
Finance, Competitiveness, and Innovation	Paulo Correa, Ana Paula Cusolito, Francesca de Nicola, Natalie Nicolaou, Arabela Sena Aprahamian, Madalina Pruna
Governance	David Bulman, Alina Mungiu-Pippidi, Irina Doroftei, Ismail Radwan, Emmaline Holland Gayk Burduja
Health, Nutrition, and Population	Marcelo Bortman, Kate Mandeville, Cristina Petcu
Macroeconomics, Trade, and Investment	Catalin Pauna, Donato De Rosa, Vincent De Paul Tsoungui Belinga, Andrei Silviu Dospinescu, Guillermo Carlos Arenas, Graciela Miralles Murciego, Hania Sahnoun, Giuseppe Russo, Ron Hood
Poverty and Equity	Yeon Soo Kim, Jonathan Karver, Gabriela Inchauste
Social Protection and Labor	Manuel Salazar, Vlad Grigoras, Sandor Karacsony, Mitchell Wiener, Alina Petric
Social, Urban, Rural, and Resilience	Alanna Simpson, Marcel Ionescu-Heroiu, Adina Dorina Vintan, Valerie Morrica
Transport and Digital Development	Jean-Francois Marteau, Nadia Badea
Water	Philippe Marin
Gender	Miriam Muller, Ana Maria Munoz Boudet
International Finance Corporation	Aimilios Chatzinikolaou, Alexander James Cantor, Cristian Nacu, Andreia Daniela Radu
Multilateral Investment Guarantee Agency	Gianfilippo Carboni

The team would like to thank our counterparts in the government of Romania, the private sector, academia and civil society, members of the World Bank Romania Country Team from all the World Bank Global Practices, and the IFC, who have contributed to the preparation of this report and participated in several rounds of extensive consultation events. We benefited greatly from their expertise and input in various forms. Maria-Magdalena Manea and Cathy Gagnet edited the report, Victor Neagu provided communications support, and Raluca Marina Banioti and Mismake D. Galatis supported the team throughout the process.

Abbreviations

ANAR	Romanian Waters National Administration
ANI	National Integrity Agency
AROP	at risk of poverty
CANE	Classification of Activities from National Economy
CF	Cohesion Fund
ECTHR	European Court of Human Rights
EIB	European Investment Bank
EPO	European Patent Office
ERDF	European Regional Development Fund
FDI	foreign direct investment
GAD	General Anticorruption Directorate
GDP	gross domestic product
GVC	global value chains
ICT	information and communications technology
MOT	Ministry of Transport
MSII	Minimum Social Insertion Income
MSME	micro, small, and medium enterprises
NEET	neither in employment nor in education and training
PISA	Program for International Student Assessment
PMR	Product Market Regulation
PPP	public-private partnerships
R&D	research and development
SCD	Systematic Country Diagnostic
SMEs	small and medium enterprises
SOE	state-owned enterprise
TFP	total factor productivity
UNFCCC	United Nations Framework Convention on Climate Change
VAT	value-added-tax
VET	vocational and educational training

Executive Summary

Romania's transformation has been "a tale of two Romanias"—one urban, dynamic, and integrated with the EU; the other rural, poor, and isolated. The reforms spurred by EU accession boosted productivity and integrated Romania into the EU economic space. GDP per capita rose from 30 percent of the EU average in 1995 to 59 percent in 2016. Today, more than 70 percent of the country's exports go to the EU, and their technological complexity is increasing rapidly. Yet Romania remains the country in the EU with by far the largest share of poor people, with more than a quarter of the population living on less than $5.50 a day (2011 purchasing power parity). There are widening disparities in economic opportunity and poverty, across regions and between urban and rural areas. While Bucharest has exceeded the EU average income per capita, and many secondary cities are becoming hubs of prosperity and innovation, Romania remains one of the least urbanized countries in the EU. Access to public services remains constrained for many citizens, particularly in rural areas, and there is a large infrastructure gap. This is a drag on the international competitiveness of the more dynamic Romania; and it limits economic opportunities for the other Romania in lagging and rural areas.

An oscillating approach to reforms lies at the root of Romania's lack of shared prosperity. Economic growth since 1990 has been among the most volatile in the EU, largely because of the hesitant approach to structural reforms, with periods of enthusiasm alternating with periods of stagnation and even reform reversal. Growth often had a narrow base, and was driven by consumption. Weak commitment to fiscal discipline frequently led to macroeconomic imbalances that required sharp subsequent corrections. Moreover, owing to poorly targeted social safety nets, the cost of the adjustments was disproportionately borne by the most vulnerable people. As a result, poverty rates have remained distinctively high given Romania's income level, and social disparities have continued to widen.

Institutional challenges must be addressed to bridge the gap between the two Romanias. Growth is constrained by weak commitment to policy implementation, creating a poor business environment and the misallocation of resources to politically connected firms. Equal opportunities are constrained by weak local service delivery and an inability to ensure sufficient local funding because of patronage-based politics. Resilience to natural disasters and climate change is constrained by lack of coordination between central and local authorities. As argued in this report, Romania has no choice but to address these institutional challenges if it is to sustain the impressive growth performance of recent years, share prosperity among all its citizens, and improve its resilience to natural hazards.

SUSTAINING GROWTH

Sustained growth depends on increasing the quantity and quality of labor and capital, as well as on improving economic efficiency. After witnessing a sharp output collapse following the global financial crisis, in recent years Romania has become one of the fastest growing economies in Europe. Yet, the quality of growth has deteriorated, with labor productivity growth slowing from 8.5 percent on average before the crisis to an annual average of about 2.5 percent after the crisis—the largest drop in Central Europe. To sustain growth in the medium term and keep converging with the living standards of Europe, Romania needs to revamp the drivers of growth, with more and better labor, better capital investment, and more efficient allocation of resources.

Labor force participation is too low to mitigate the effects of aging and emigration. Between 2000 and 2017, Romania's population fell from 22.8 to 19.6 million, and is expected to continue falling. With an estimated 3 to 5 million Romanians living and working abroad, in 2010 Romania ranked as the tenth main country of origin of migration flows in the G20, with highly educated emigrants accounting for 26.6 percent of the total. The shrinking quantity of labor is not compensated for by greater labor force participation, which—with an overall rate of 68.8 percent and 60.2 percent for women in 2017—is one of the lowest in the EU.

The skills of the workforce are inadequate for the needs of a modern economy. Over the last two decades, Romania's economy has become increasingly sophisticated, with its exports switching from labor-intensive, low-technology sectors to more advanced sectors like automotive, machinery, and electronic equipment. The skills of the workforce are struggling to keep up with the needs of a more sophisticated economy. Tertiary education attainment, at 25.6 percent in 2016, is the lowest in the EU, and Romania lags in the number of graduates in STEM disciplines. Skills shortages are also reported in skilled manual occupations, partially reflecting the low development of vocational training, and key socio-emotional skills are found to be particularly lacking.

Private investment has remained at fairly high levels, but a shallow financial sector limits the availability of long-term finance. Romania invested, on average, 25 percent of GDP between 2000 and 2016, mostly in manufacturing and nonresidential construction, with private sector investment accounting for more than 75 percent of the total. However, foreign direct investment (FDI) inflows—a conduit for the transfer of capital, access to modern technologies, competition, and better managerial skills—remain below precrisis levels. The banking sector is the main financial intermediary, but bank loans to private enterprises amount to a meagre 12.7 percent of GDP. Overall, a shallow and bank-centric financial sector limits the availability of long-term finance for investment.

Public investment has not played a supportive role because of institutional weaknesses. Romania ranks 102nd out of 137 countries in the quality of its transport infrastructure, according to the World Economic Forum's *Global Competitiveness Report 2017–2018*. Clearly, high levels of public investment, boosted by the large influx of EU funds since EU accession in 2007, have not yielded the expected results in terms of quality and quantity of transport infrastructure. Insufficient institutional coordination, ineffective policy implementation and monitoring, politicization of decision making, poor human resources policies in public administration, and delays in implementing results-based budgeting have contributed to weak public investment performance.

An unpredictable business environment and the large presence of state-owned enterprises (SOEs) in the economy undermine the efficient allocation of resources. Key factors behind the slowdown in productivity since 2008 include access to credit and red tape. The unpredictability of the business environment—a direct consequence of institutional failures—is a significant challenge to business operations. For example, in recent years, businesses were faced with many fiscal measures introduced, and then reversed, which severely impacted their ability to plan operations, including investments. According to the European Investment Bank (EIB) investment survey 2016, "political and regulatory climate" was the top factor negatively impacting firms' ability to carry out planned investment for 47 percent of Romanian firms. Poor corporate governance of SOEs is another source of inefficiency, dragging down aggregate productivity both directly in the sectors where SOEs are active, and indirectly through the inefficient provision of inputs to other sectors of the economy.

SHARING PROSPERITY

Romania's prosperity is not equally shared, as the bottom 40 is largely disconnected from the drivers of growth. Close to half of the people at the bottom 40 percent of the income distribution do not work, and another 28 percent remain engaged in subsistence agriculture. Improvements in income before the crisis were driven by a large-scale labor reallocation from agriculture to low-skilled sectors, but those gains were reversed as the same sectors shed large numbers of jobs during the crisis. Poverty is highly concentrated in rural areas, where the labor force is highly unskilled and where there are few opportunities. Low internal mobility further reinforces Romania's dual development challenge—less than 2 percent of the population reports having moved in the past five years, implying that structural constraints inhibit internal mobility toward economic opportunities. Lack of institutional commitments to long-term policies—and an inability to ensure sufficient local funding as a result of patronage-based politics—are at the core of slow and uneven progress in meeting the human capital challenges. They also inhibit other reforms that could alleviate structural constraints to job growth and improve the effectiveness of the social protection system.

Inequality in opportunities persists, holding up transitions to more productive jobs and widening the human capital gap. Forty percent of 15-year-old Romanian students are functionally illiterate; and early school-leaving—at 18.5 percent—is one of the highest in the EU. The health care system is overregulated, creating barriers in access to services, and a weak primary care system disproportionately affects the poor and vulnerable. The challenge is particularly severe for the Roma people, who have a 28 percent employment rate and a staggeringly high poverty rate of 70 percent. Maintaining a focus on equal opportunities, targeting efforts to reach marginalized communities, and enhancing mobility through infrastructure investments can substantially increase the potential for agglomeration and more effectively reduce regional disparities.

Improvements in the labor market have been slow, constraining productive employment. A broader labor shortage exists amid the low labor force participation of key demographic groups. Existing labor market and family policies reinforce the low participation rate of women, as strong gender norms continue to place the burden of child and elderly care on women. And a large share of the workforce is trapped in low-productivity agricultural and other informal activities, leading to the underutilization and misallocation of labor. Reducing rural poverty requires tackling the large agricultural productivity gap caused by fragmented farm structures and low access to credit and extension services. Meanwhile, relatively few in the bottom 40 hold formal jobs that would benefit from minimum wage increases, but the potential cost of the policy could be high if it is not accompanied by corresponding increases in labor productivity.

Equity requires a robust social safety net for those falling behind and high-quality public services for all. Social spending is the second-lowest in the EU, at 14.4 percent of GDP. It is also inefficient and increasingly skewed toward pensions. This makes it less effective at reaching the people most in need, as pension coverage among the rural poor is low and falling. The provision of social services that involve social protection, employment, education, and healthcare is fragmented and sparse, especially in rural areas where the need is the greatest. Formalizing property rights could provide the foundation for boosting private sector activities, including the development of agribusinesses, and could promote spatial development and public infrastructure. Improving access to public services remains an urgent priority, as 22 percent of the population still lack access to potable water and 32 percent live without a flush toilet. Most of the gap is in rural areas.

IMPROVING RESILIENCE

Natural hazards pose a great challenge to the Romanian economy and disproportionately affect the poor. Romania stands out for its vulnerability to risks from earthquakes, floods, and droughts, the latter two intensified by climate change. These disaster risks disproportionately affect poorer counties. The potential damage to natural, physical, and human assets can curtail economic growth, jeopardize fiscal sustainability, and negatively affect the well-being of Romania's population. Improving resilience to natural disasters will require institutional efforts on disaster preparedness and risk reduction, and the mainstreaming of climate change in policy considerations.

STRENGTHENING INSTITUTIONS

Despite progress, particularly in judicial anti-corruption work, fundamental institutions remain weak and constrain progress in inclusive growth. Reforms stemming from the EU accession process have not resulted in transformative institutional improvements. Past top-down efforts have not alleviated deeper systemic problems, as corruption is a consequence of deep-rooted systemic deficiencies in state behavior and in state–society interactions.

Functional challenges hinder inclusive growth and resilience. The public sector struggles to credibly commit to reforms and policy implementation, which creates a difficult environment for firms. This is evidenced by the frequent use of "emergency ordinances" and frequent changes to fiscal legislation. Weak commitment to deliver on long-term objectives undermines service delivery and equality of opportunity. Fragmentation of sectoral responsibilities has led to poor inter-sectoral coordination and diffuse accountability, further limited by poor access to information. The most notable example of weak coordination is found in deep inefficiencies in public spending and bottlenecks in the absorption of EU funds. Corruption undermines cooperation and trust in the state, leading to citizen disengagement.

Underlying power asymmetries cause corruption and poor governance. The causes of these challenges can be traced back to state capture by vested interests and a pervasive clientelism that leads to resource misallocation—as seen in public procurement contracts—and that limits innovation. Clientelism and patronage in the civil service undermine public sector capacity. The civil service remains highly politicized, while the nonmeritocratic system leads to a lack of trust and weakens the innovation ecosystem.

Given the complex governance challenges, increasing transparency to enhance accountability would be an important step to improve implementation capacity and oversight. Developing a management framework for public investment for both budgetary and EU funds could significantly improve the predictability of fiscal policies and public investment efficiency. Further, reducing bureaucratic requirements could help shift anticorruption efforts toward prevention and return trust in the state. Reforming the civil service by depoliticizing public administration and creating professional senior management would reduce the bottlenecks in decision making.

The key lesson from this diagnostic is that despite impressive economic growth, achieving shared prosperity and sustainable welfare improvements will remain a distant reality if Romania does not address its governance challenges. Identifying governance failures as the binding development constraint sheds light on why economic growth continues to be volatile and noninclusive. Concerted efforts are needed to enhance commitment to long-term policy goals, while future policies need to acknowledge and address the underlying institutional challenges. Resolving these will be a long and difficult process, but the potential rewards will be high. This would also help Romania counter the consequences of a shrinking and aging population, and allow those at the bottom to contribute more actively to economic growth, which could trigger a virtuous cycle of inclusive growth and development.

REFORM PRIORITIES FOR INCLUSIVE GROWTH

This Systematic Country Diagnostic (SCD) proposes a number of development priorities for Romania that will help enhance equity and shared prosperity. Four broad areas of priority are identified: (i) increase the effectiveness and efficiency of the state in public service delivery; (ii) catalyze private sector growth and competitiveness; (iii) ensure equal opportunities for all; and (iv) build resilience for sustainable growth. The governance priorities are considered as prerequisites, whereas the other three areas proposed are intended to be complementary and mutually supportive. The complete list of priorities is very long, as difficult challenges remain in many key areas. Priorities are identified based on their potential for reducing poverty, boosting shared prosperity, and advancing toward the goal. A table with a detailed list of priorities is presented in Chapter 6. These priorities will inform the World Bank Group's engagement in Romania for the period 2019–2023.

1 A Tale of Two Romanias

Romania's transformation has been a tale of two Romanias: one urban, dynamic, and integrated with the EU; the other rural, poor, and isolated. Reforms spurred by EU accession boosted productivity and integrated Romania into the EU economic space. GDP per capita rose from 30 percent of the EU average in 1995 to 59 percent in 2016. Today, more than 70 percent of the country's exports go to the EU, and their technological complexity is increasing rapidly. Internet speed is among the fastest in the world and the gross value added of the information and communications technology (ICT) sector in GDP, at 5.9 percent in 2016, is among the highest in the EU. Yet Romania remains the country in the Union with by far the largest share of poor people, when measured by the $5.50 per day poverty line (2011 purchasing power parity) (figure 1.1). More than a quarter of the population—26 percent in 2015—lives on less than $5.50 a day. This is more than double the rate for Bulgaria (12 percent). There are widening disparities in economic opportunity and poverty across regions and between urban and rural areas. While Bucharest has already exceeded the EU average income per capita and many secondary cities are becoming hubs of prosperity and innovation, Romania remains one of the least urbanized countries in the EU, with only 55 percent of people living in cities. Overall, access to public services remains constrained for many citizens, particularly in rural areas, and there is a large infrastructure gap, which is a drag on the international competitiveness of the more dynamic Romania and limits economic opportunities for the other Romania in lagging and rural areas.

Romania's dual development is a manifestation of a lack of shared prosperity and the result of institutional failures, which lie at the root of the volatile and not sufficiently inclusive growth of the past three decades. Economic growth since 1990 has been among the most volatile in the EU, largely as a result of the hesitant approach to structural reforms, with periods of enthusiasm alternating with periods of stagnation and even reform reversal. Growth often had a narrow base and was driven by consumption. Weak commitment to fiscal discipline frequently led to macroeconomic imbalances that required sharp subsequent corrections. Moreover, owing to poorly targeted social safety nets, the cost of the adjustments was disproportionately borne by the most vulnerable. As a result,

FIGURE 1.1

Romania has by far the largest share of poor people in the EU

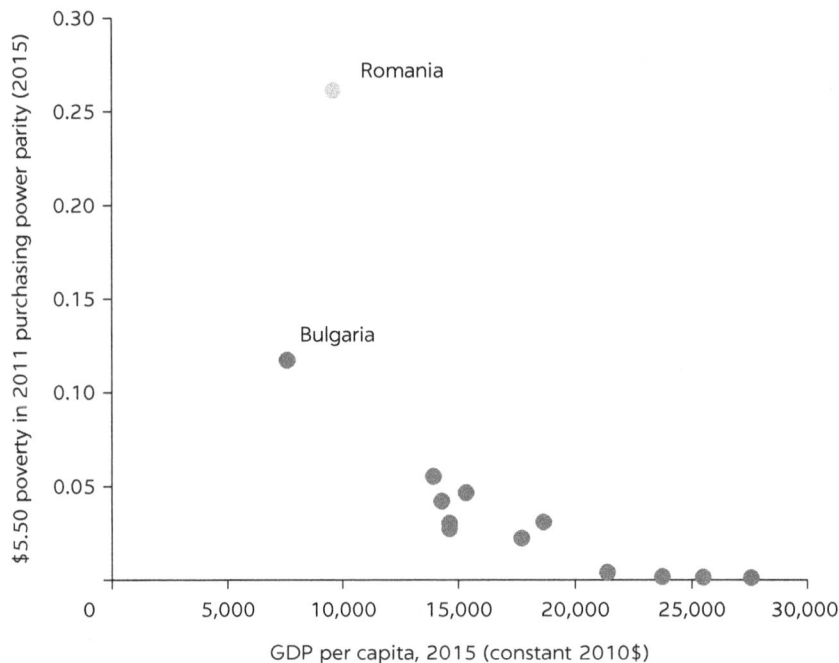

Source: World Bank calculation based on World Development Indicators.

poverty rates have remained distinctively high for Romania's income level, and social disparities have been widening.

In the first phase of transition, institutional legacies from the old order led to a late start of reforms, while the opening of the economy led to a large contraction in output and rapidly increasing inequality. In the early 1990s, prices were liberalized and the legal framework for private property and a market-based economy was established. Often guided by the desire to protect powerful vested interests, the authorities tried to preserve employment in the state-owned enterprise (SOE) sector and in the public administration, hampering the development of private enterprise and the reallocation of labor to more productive jobs. Consequently, real wages declined as productivity stagnated and inflation surged. Voucher-based mass privatization was launched in 1995, with limited success. The adoption of an early retirement program in 1994 led to a significant drop in employment. Low job creation led to long-term unemployment, with ensuing high external migration, and agriculture became the employer of last resort. Income disparities deteriorated rapidly, and the Gini inequality index increased from 0.2 to 0.3 in a decade.

The run-up to EU accession in 2007 provided an anchor for institutional transformation, but growth remained uneven and inequality continued to worsen. Romania was invited to open negotiations with the EU in December 1999. Until Romania joined in January 2007, EU accession remained an anchor for reforms, providing momentum for the privatization and restructuring of SOEs and for regulatory and judiciary reforms. Output gradually recovered, and until 2008 the country enjoyed high but volatile growth. Productivity increased as foreign direct investment (FDI) began to come into the manufacturing sector, bringing new technologies, modern processes, and access to external markets.

Unemployment was on a declining trend, but youth and long-term unemployment remained elevated. Skills and labor shortages became increasingly widespread. High inactivity persisted stubbornly, particularly among women. Gains in labor force participation were modest overall. While there were important improvements in the well-being of the population, stark differences remained across social groups and regions of the country, and between urban and rural areas. Inequality increased further, as large categories of people—the Roma in particular—continued to be excluded from the benefits of growth.

Although output has recovered since 2008, institutional shortcomings have compounded the effects of the crisis, contributing to significant setbacks in poverty reduction, and are again leading to macroeconomic imbalances. In the run-up to the 2008 crisis, pro-cyclical fiscal policies and sizeable capital inflows caused widening macroeconomic imbalances, leading to a 7.1 percent contraction in GDP in 2009 (figure 1.2). This caused large-scale job losses, with many of the poor falling back on agriculture as a means of last resort. The construction sector, which contributed significantly to job growth before the crisis, was hit particularly hard, and job creation in low-skilled sectors has been modest since then. Fiscal consolidation during 2009–2015 has helped place economic growth on a strong footing. However, lack of commitment and underfunding for the delivery of public services and poor targeting of social programs have contributed to the negative income growth of the bottom 40 percent of the income distribution (the so-called bottom 40) in 2009–2015, with poverty remaining above precrisis levels, and inequality still among the highest in the EU (figure 1.3). Furthermore, since 2016, a wavering commitment to fiscal

FIGURE 1.2

Output contracted significantly in 2009 and recovery has been slow

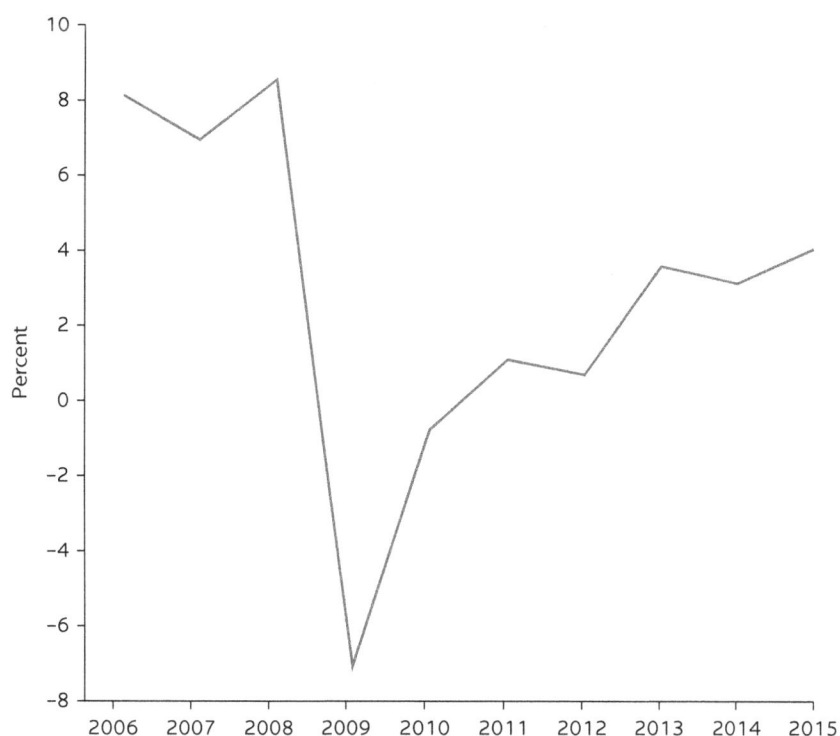

Source: World Development Indicators.

FIGURE 1.3

Poverty rates have not reverted to precrisis levels and inequality remains entrenched

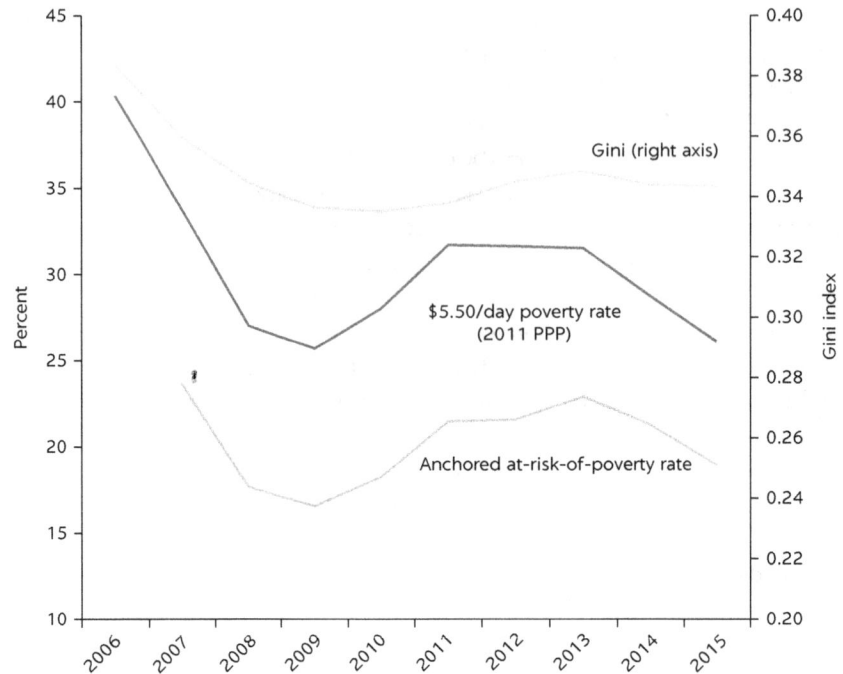

Source: Eurostat, World Bank staff calculation using EU-SILC.
Note: PPP = purchasing power parity.

discipline has led to widening macroeconomic imbalances, again exposing Romania to the risks of future shocks.

The process of institutional convergence with the EU remains incomplete, and the poor functioning of institutions is at the root of Romania's dual development. EU accession led to substantial *de jure* reforms, which were often subsequently reversed or weakly implemented. As a result, Romania still performs below European averages in many key areas of governance, including government effectiveness, voice and accountability, regulatory quality, and political stability. While important steps have been taken to address corruption, citizens still perceive it as high and widespread. An incomplete institutional transition and high political volatility over the past 25 years have reduced the trust in the state, effectively undermining the social contract. This has limited the government's ability to implement important public policies to boost the economy's growth potential, create equal opportunities and jobs for all citizens, and improve the country's resilience to natural disasters.

Governance challenges must be addressed to bridge the gap between the two Romanias and converge with the high-income EU. Growth is constrained by weak commitment to policy implementation, creating a poor business environment and the misallocation of resources to politically connected firms. Equal opportunities for the poor and bottom 40 are constrained by weak local service delivery and an inability to ensure sufficient local funding because of patronage-based politics. Resilience to natural disasters and climate change is constrained by a lack of coordination between central and local authorities. As will be illustrated in the coming chapters, Romania has no choice but to address these challenges if it is to achieve sustainable and inclusive growth.

2 Easing Supply-Side Constraints to Growth

TO ACHIEVE HIGH-INCOME STATUS, ROMANIA NEEDS TO BOOST ITS GROWTH POTENTIAL

Romania is one of the fastest-growing economies in the EU, but growth has increasingly been driven by consumption and has produced widening macroeconomic imbalances. Economic growth has accelerated in the last two years, driven mostly by a sharp increase in private consumption on the back of resumed fiscal expansion and increases in minimum wages. Real GDP grew 4.8 percent in 2016 and 6.9 percent in 2017. At the same time, investment as a share of GDP has been on a declining trend since 2008, reaching 22.6 in 2017. Since 2016, pro-cyclical fiscal policies have widened the government deficit to nearly 3 percent of GDP, and public debt in ESA terms—albeit among the lowest in the EU at 35 percent of GDP at the end of 2017—is not stabilized at current deficit levels. Inflation is on an upward trend and has reached 4.95 percent in early 2018, while the current account deficit widened to 3.4 percent of GDP at end-2017 (see appendix).

Achieving the average living standards of Europe requires increasing the economy's growth potential. Romania's speed of convergence to the average income levels of the EU has been impressive, while the composition of its national wealth has been changing (box 2.1 and World Bank 2018d). Yet, with 5 percent annual GDP growth it would still take Romania 19 years to reach the average living standards of the EU–28 (figure 2.1). But 5 percent is substantially higher than the 3.1 percent average GDP growth achieved in 2005–2016, making it imperative to increase the economy's growth potential.

Boosting potential growth entails enhancing labor productivity. Labor productivity growth has slowed from 8.5 percent on average before the crisis to an annual average of about 2.5 percent—the largest drop in Central Europe—after the crisis (figure 2.2). The precrisis strong labor productivity growth helped the country to reduce the gap with the EU by more than one-third in 8 years (from 76 percentage points in 2000 to 50 percentage points in 2008). The sluggish productivity growth postcrisis delayed the convergence toward EU levels, with the productivity gap declining by only ¼ in the postcrisis period (from 50 in 2008 to 37.5 percentage points in 2016).

FIGURE 2.1

Romania's convergence with the EU–28 is still some way off

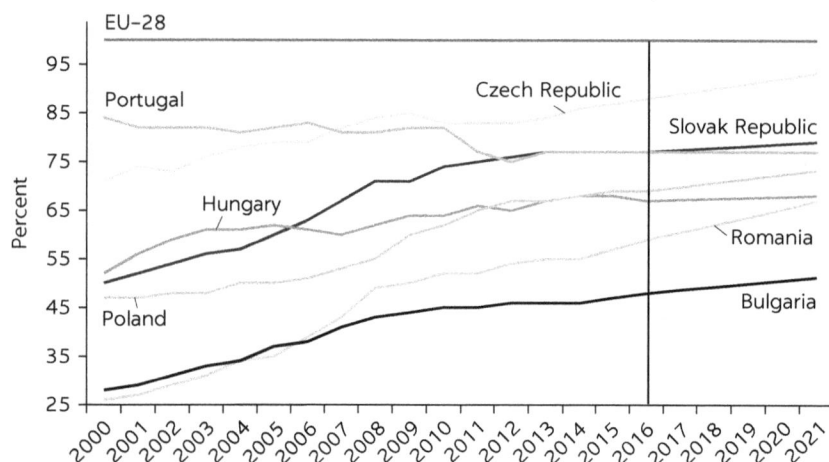

Source: Eurostat, projections 2017–20 based on the last five-year growth average.

Number of years to achieve convergence with EU–28

ROMANIA'S GROWTH RATE (%)	NUMBER OF YEARS
5	19
6	14
7	11
8	9

Source: World Bank calculations based on Eurostat data on GDP per capita in purchasing power standards.
Note: Annual growth rate of EU–28 is equal to EU–28 last five-year growth average.

BOX 2.1

An alternative way to measure Romania's economic performance: wealth accounting

The common measure of economic growth is gross domestic product (GDP). However, GDP looks at only one part of economic performance—income as a flow—and says nothing about the wealth and assets that underlie this income (the stock). This is analogous to measuring a company's performance by only looking at its income statement (sales) and not its balance sheet, which includes income, assets, and liabilities for a more complete picture of its overall sustainability. Total wealth is the sum of produced capital, human capital, and natural capital (plus net foreign assets).

Romania's per capita total wealth is comparable within the upper middle-income group globally, but it is substantially lower than the regional average for Europe and Central Asia, and that of its neighbors. For 2014, Romania's total wealth was estimated at $2.1 trillion, and per capita wealth at $107,000.

Romania's total wealth per capita is slightly lower than other countries in its income group, where the average for upper middle-income countries is $114,000; but it is substantially lower than its regional average, which is about $368,000 for Europe and Central Asia. Romania is also at the lower end when compared to its Eastern European peers (figure B2.1.1).

Total wealth in Romania has been growing over time, with greater contributions from produced and human capital, but less from natural capital. Total wealth grew 24 percent from 1995 to 2014, but its composition also changed (figure B2.1.2). Produced capital (including urban land) grew 67 percent and now represents 38 percent of total wealth. Human capital grew by 34 percent and now represents 50 percent of total wealth. Conversely, natural capital decreased 24 percent from 1995 to 2014, and now only represents 16 percent of total wealth.

(continued)

BOX 2.1, *continued*

FIGURE B2.1.1

Romania's per capita total wealth is lower than in selected peer countries

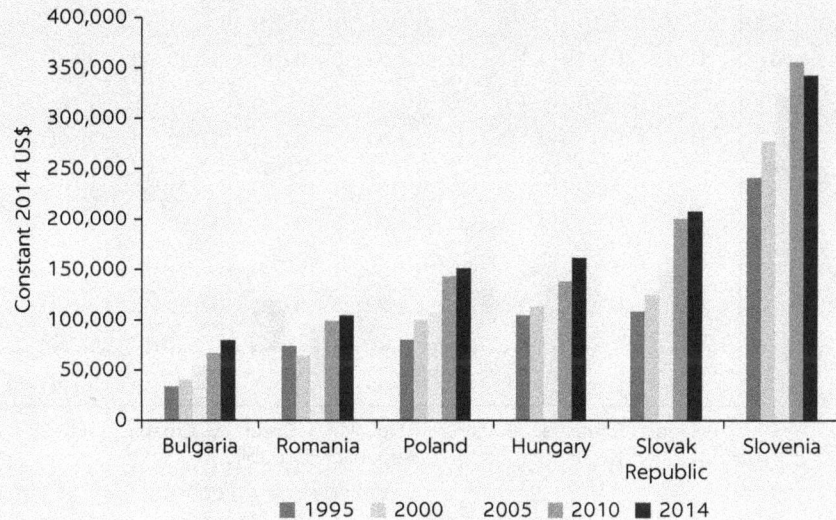

Source: World Bank 2016.

FIGURE B2.1.2

The share of natural capital in Romania has been shrinking over time

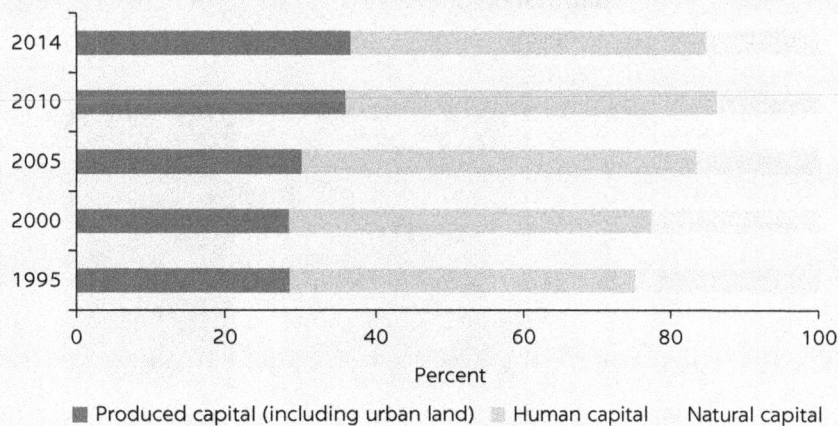

Source: https://datacatalog.worldbank.org/dataset/wealth-accounting

Sustained growth depends on increasing the quantity and quality of labor and capital, and on improving economic efficiency. The drivers of Romania's GDP growth have been gradually changing since 2000 (figure 2.3). In 2000–2008 the bulk of economic growth (80 percent) was associated with total factor productivity (TFP), reflecting the efficiency gains from the gradual correction of resource misallocation during the transition to a market economy. Positive contributions were also made by physical capital (38 percent) and human capital (3 percent), while a sizeable negative contribution resulted from labor

FIGURE 2.2

Since 2008 Romania has experienced a large decline in labor productivity growth

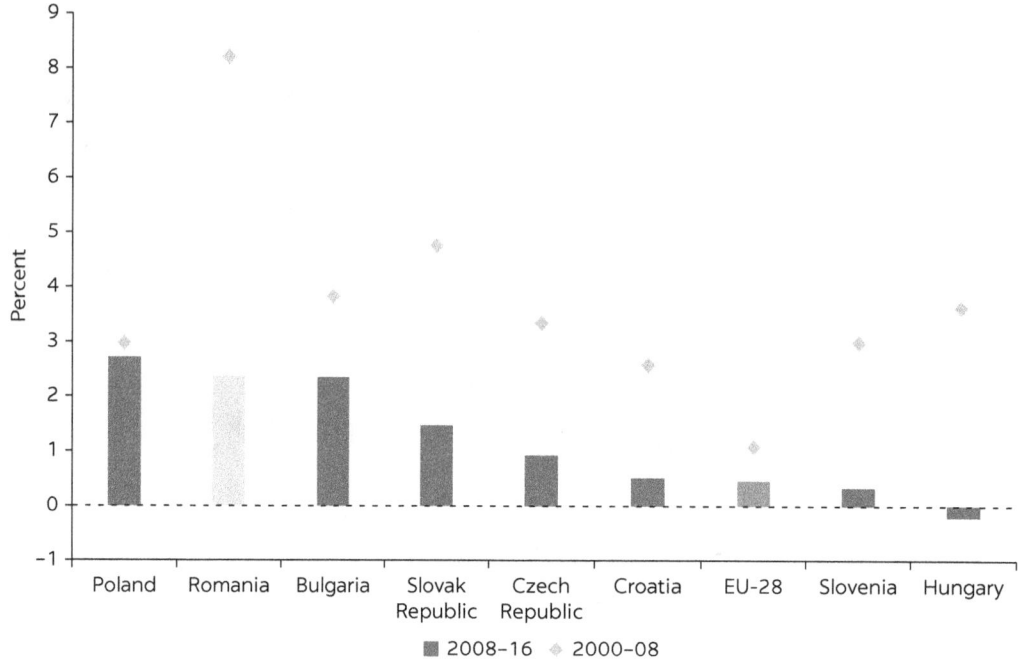

Source: Eurostat.

FIGURE 2.3

Since 2008 the sources of growth have shifted with a reduced contribution of TFP

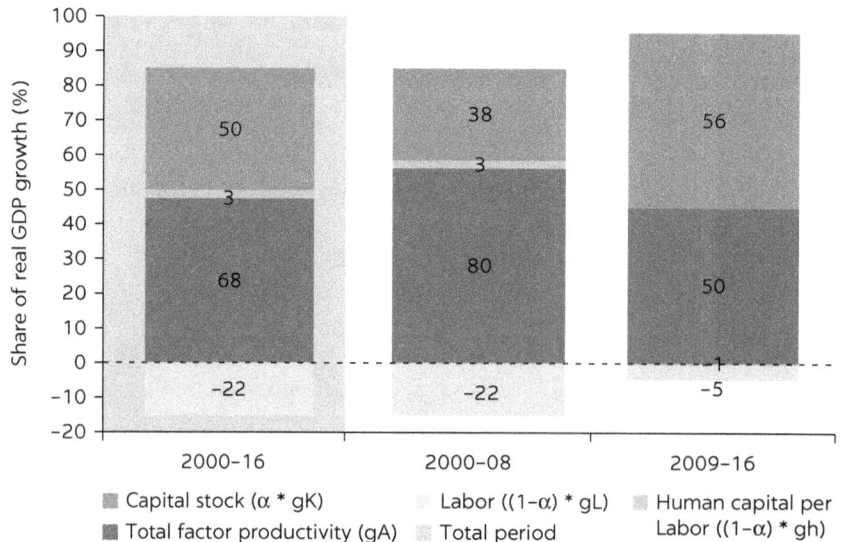

Sources: Eurostat and World Bank calculations, based on a human capital adjusted Solow model.

(−22 percent). Since 2009, the sources of growth have shifted, with a reduction of the TFP contribution (to 50 percent), an increase in the contribution of physical capital (to 56 percent) and a negative contribution of labor and human capital. The remainder of this chapter examines the role of labor, capital, and total factor productivity as drivers of growth.

BROADER LABOR FORCE PARTICIPATION AND ADEQUATE SKILLS WILL HELP SUSTAIN GROWTH

Declining fertility and emigration are contributing to an aging and shrinking population.[1] Romania's total and working age populations declined by about 3.6 and 2.2 million, respectively, between 1990 and 2017, and are expected to continue falling. Romania's fertility rate declined from 1.8 in 1990 to the current 1.6, while the age structure has shifted with the share of population aged 65+ increasing from 10.3 to 17.4 percent. Between 3 and 5 million Romanians currently live and work abroad, mostly in OECD and European countries.[2] Between 2000 and 2017, Romania's population fell from 22.8 to 19.6 million, with outward migration accounting for more than 75 percent of this decline.[3] Moreover, Romanian working-age emigrants in OECD countries may exceed 2.6 million (OECD and UN–DESA 2013), representing over 76 percent of Romanian emigrants and about 20 percent of the Romanian total working population.

In the 2000s, Romania experienced one of the largest brain drains globally. According to OECD (2017), in 2010 Romania ranked as the tenth main country of origin of the migration flows in the G20. In terms of high-skilled immigration into the G20 countries, Romania recorded the largest increase in the first decade of the 2000s, reaching a stock of about 492,000 persons in 2010–11. The share of highly educated emigrants in total emigrants was also high, at 23 percent as of 2010—the second highest among the top countries of origin. This has had important consequences for the labor market and for the contribution of labor and human capital to the potential growth of the Romanian economy, especially in the private sector. For example, the number of physicians working abroad exceeded 14,000 as of 2013, representing more than 26 percent of the total number of Romanian physicians. As will be argued in Chapter 5, brain drain is one of the forms of "citizen exit," motivated by lack of trust and by the belief that talent will not be adequately rewarded owing to the lack of meritocracy.

Romania's labor force participation rate is one of the lowest in the EU, resulting from the weak participation of women and lower-educated people in the labor market. In 2000, Romania's labor force participation rate was about 69.1 percent, above the EU average of 66.6 percent. In 2017, it had dropped to 68.8 percent, one of the lowest in the EU. The participation rate is particularly low for women and for people with lower levels of education. While about 77.3 percent of men were active in the labor market in 2017, only 60.2 percent of women were. The participation rate for people with tertiary education was 90.1 percent, compared with 72.3 percent for people with upper secondary education, and only 58.7 percent for people with educational levels below upper secondary.

There are shortages in key occupations, including ICT, health, and education, as well as science and engineering professionals and technicians (European Commission 2014). Beyond the emigration of highly skilled labor, institutional shortcomings in the Romanian education system have led to insufficient numbers of highly skilled workers. Tertiary education attainment (30–34 years old) has not increased since 2015, and has remained at 25.6 percent in 2016—the lowest in the EU. While Romania's target of 26.7 percent by 2020 is achievable, this remains a low percentage compared with the EU average of 39.1 percent in 2016 and the EU 2020 target of 40 percent (figure 2.4). Romania also lags among peers in the number of graduate students per population aged 20–29 in STEM[4] disciplines (figure 2.5). Skills shortages also exist in skilled manual occupational groups, including machinery mechanics and repairers; cooks; car, van, and

FIGURE 2.4

Tertiary education attainment (30–34-years-old) is the lowest among EU countries

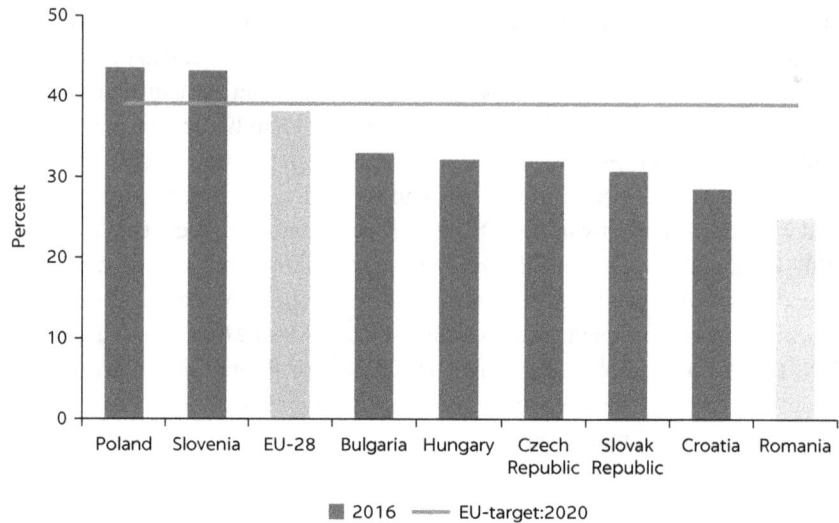

Source: Eurostat.

FIGURE 2.5

Tertiary education outcome in STEM disciplines is among the lowest

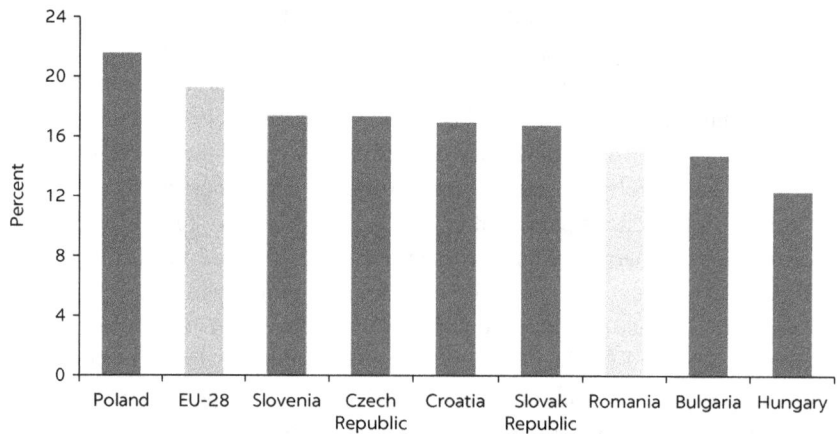

Source: Eurostat.

motorcycle drivers; and workers in garment and related trades, partially reflecting the low development of vocational training or technical school education.[5] Difficulties in finding skilled staff have important implications for private sector growth.

The shortage of highly skilled labor is made worse by skills mismatches in the labor market and by the low participation of adults in lifelong learning. According to Romanian employers, current employees, students, and graduates entering the labor market lack key socio-emotional skills (motivation, empathy, tolerance, self-management, problem-solving, teamwork, communication, learning to learn, accountability, planning, engagement, and commitment).[6] At the same time, university graduates are perceived to possess sufficient, though overly theoretical, academic skills, while vocational and educational training (VET) students or graduates have outdated skills because of outdated equipment in school workshops, as well as outdated teaching methods and teaching experiences. In many countries, including Romania, the automation of production processes is driving the demand for higher levels of cognitive skills.[7] This change will displace large numbers of workers whose jobs involve the routine application of procedural knowledge.[8] Finally, at 1.2 percent, adult participation in learning remains very low in Romania compared with the EU average of 10.8 percent, at a time when there is an important need for upskilling.

PRIVATE INVESTMENT HAS HELPED REBUILD THE CAPITAL STOCK, BUT MORE EFFICIENT PUBLIC INVESTMENT IS NEEDED TO ADDRESS THE INFRASTRUCTURE GAP

Romania invested, on average, 25 percent of its GDP between 2000 and 2016, most of it in manufacturing and nonresidential construction. Capital stock has significantly contributed to Romania's potential growth (figure 2.3). Private sector investment accounted for more than 75 percent of total investment (figure 2.6), and equipment and nonresidential construction accounted for more than

FIGURE 2.6

Investment has been sizeable, driven by the private sector

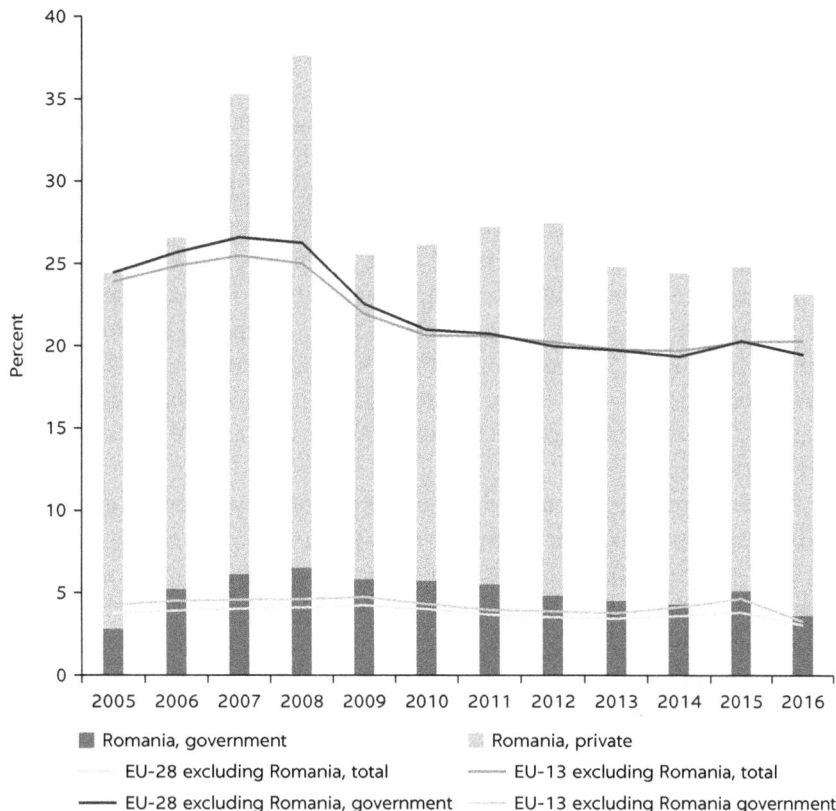

Source: European Commission.

FIGURE 2.7

The bulk of investment has been allocated to equipment and nonresidential construction

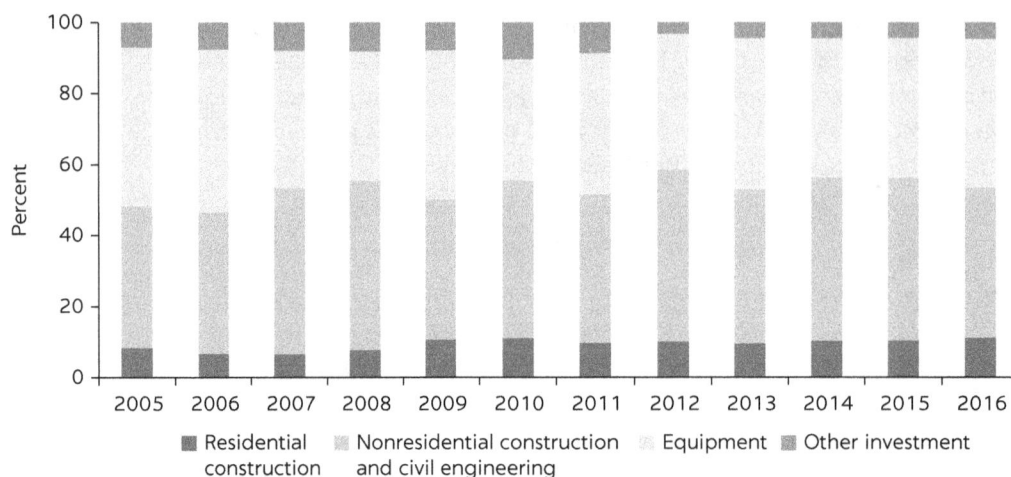

Source: AMECO Database.

80 percent (figure 2.7) of the private sector investment. The recent impressive economic growth has also had a positive spillover on the enterprise sector, with more than 31 percent of businesses reporting an increase in their turnover of more than 20 percent over the last 3 years. Increased turnover has been accompanied by an increase in investment activity, with the percentage of firms that invested rising from 60 percent in 2014 to 67.5 percent in 2015—which is still low compared with Poland's 78.8 percent.

The banking sector is the main financial intermediary, but it is shallow and declining. Access to credit for the private sector remains limited, potentially slowing firms' investment. Financial intermediation in Romania is low in all segments, with the banking sector accounting for 75.2 percent of financial sector assets. Banking sector assets fell from 73.7 percent of GDP in 2010 to 52.7 percent in September 2017—among the lowest in the region.[9] Low intermediation is reflected in the low penetration of both deposits and loans. The deposit base stood at 36.3 percent of GDP in September 2017, compared with an average of 71.4 percent for Bulgaria, Croatia, Hungary, and Poland, while bank loans to private enterprises reached only 12.7 percent of GDP, versus a peer average of 22.5 percent.

The development of local capital markets would allow financial deepening and improve the availability of long-term financing. Romania's capital market is the least deep in Europe. According to an index of capital markets activity in 23 sectors relative to GDP, Romania scores an index value of 16 compared to an EU average of 100.[10] Listed stock and debt securities amounted to 37.1 percent of GDP at the end of 2016, vs. 219.9 percent in the EU. The equity market, which is accessible to more established companies, is significantly smaller than regional peers, while private equity and venture capital markets are still in a nascent stage. As of end–2017, the Bucharest Stock Exchange had a market capitalization to GDP ratio of 20 percent and 87 listed companies.[11] Increasing the variety of financial instruments, including by increasing the role of nonbanking financial institutions and the introduction of covered bonds as a new asset class, would help deepen the market. Bond finance would provide healthy competition to bank loans for the financing of firms.

Net FDI inflows remain below precrisis levels. FDI has positive implications for the host country's economic growth. It stimulates transfer of capital, access to modern technologies, competition, better managerial skills, and employment. As in many countries, Romania's net FDI inflows significantly declined from a peak of 7.3 percent of GDP per year in 2004–2008[12] to an average of 2 percent in 2009–2012. Despite signs of recovery over 4 years (2013–2016), with an average of 2.3 percent of GDP per year, they are still far below the precrisis level, reflecting not only the consequences of the Global Recession, but also a deceleration of the privatization process, which reflects hesitant commitment to structural reforms.

Business investment is hampered by poor infrastructure. According to the Global Competitiveness Report 2017–2018, Romania ranks 102nd out of 137 countries in the quality of transport infrastructure, which constitutes one of the weakest areas of its business environment. Similarly, the country has the second-lowest ranking in the EU in the World Bank's Logistics Performance Index. In the European Investment Bank's (EIB) Investment Survey for 2016, availability of adequate transport infrastructure is listed as a major obstacle to long-term investment by 45 percent of Romanian firms, compared with 12.9 percent in Poland, and is the second-top-rated investment constraint, behind only the unpredictability of the business environment. In particular, Romania lags in terms of available motorways and railways relative to its population and land area. This is also true for modern transport infrastructure, captured by the relatively low share of electrified railways. As of 2015, only 42.3 percent of the total length of railway lines in Romania were electrified, compared with 63.9 percent in Poland and 53.2 percent, on average, in the EU.[13]

Relatively high public investment, boosted by the large influx of EU funds, has not yielded the expected results in terms of quality and quantity of transport infrastructure. Public investment in Romania has been substantially higher than the EU average (figure 2.6), fueled by EU funds. Between 2007 and 2013, Romania received about Euro 15.4 billion from the European Regional Development Fund (ERDF) and the Cohesion Fund (CF), an equivalent of 25.1 percent of government capital investment, with transport infrastructure among the main beneficiaries. As of March 2018, Romania had absorbed only 17 percent of the EUR 30.9 billion of EU funds allocated for the 2014–2020 programming period.[14]

Inefficient public investment is a symptom of weak public investment management. As discussed in Chapter 5, weak institutional coordination, ineffective policy implementation and monitoring, politicization of decision making, poor human resources policies in public administration, and delays in implementing results-based budgeting have contributed to weak public investment performance.

Privatization of infrastructure and public-private partnerships (PPPs) may hold significant potential in Romania. Privatization of transport infrastructure could help improve operational efficiency and sector development, while freeing up budget resources. Furthermore, PPPs in key sectors such as transport (ports, highways, and airports) and power (renewables) could bring significant financial benefits and operational efficiencies. PPPs could also be developed selectively, to improve municipal services (for example, waste) and social infrastructure. Establishing a well-structured PPP law, developing relevant institutional capacity, and tendering infrastructure projects on a competitive basis can unlock the door to private sector participation. Strong government leadership, commitment, and long-term vision are keys to the development of a PPP agenda.

EASING CONSTRAINTS TO DOING BUSINESS AND RECONSIDERING THE ROLE OF SOEs ARE THE KEYS TO SUSTAINED PRODUCTIVITY GROWTH

Romania's aggregate productivity growth slowed down substantially following the 2008 crisis, possibly driven by the declining productivity of top performing firms, mainly in services.[15] Between 2003 and 2008, Romania's GDP grew, on average, by 6.9 percent, with TFP contributing about 3.9 percentage points. Between 2008 and 2013, average annual GDP growth stood at −0.6 percent with TFP contributing −1.5 percentage points. Over the same period, firm-level data show a decline in both TFP median and dispersion for all firms and for firms in services. While a declining dispersion is a sign of reduced misallocation of resources in the economy, its occurrence together with declining median TFP suggests that top-performing firms may have become less productive.

Evidence from other sectors is mixed, with signs of increased misallocation in manufacturing and mining, but increased productivity gains in agriculture. The Increased dispersion of TFP in mining and manufacturing reflects the increasing misallocation of resources to less productive firms. At the same time, the TFP median declined, suggesting that firms at the bottom of the TFP distribution became less productive. Agriculture seems to have been more resilient, with a small increase in TFP dispersion, a sign of resource misallocation, but an increase in median TFP (figure 2.8).

FIGURE 2.8

Top firms may have become less productive

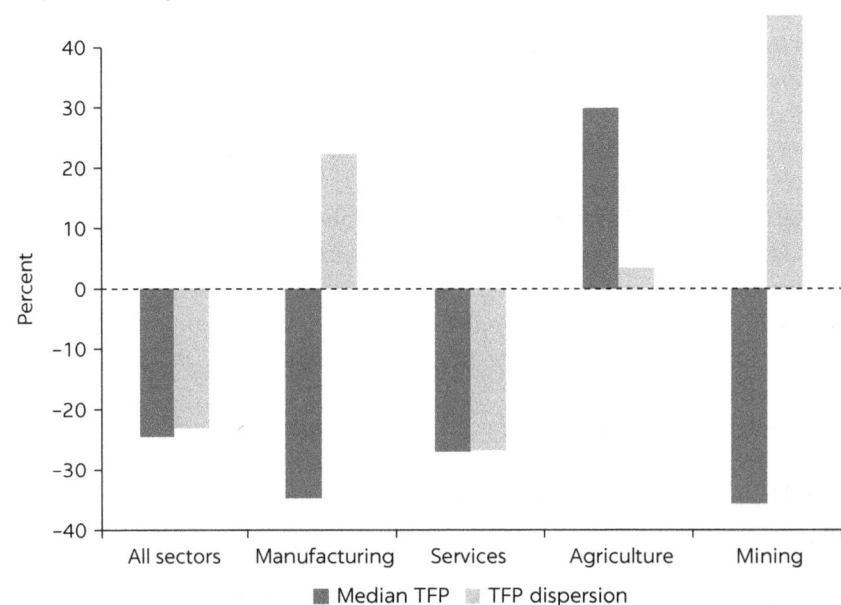

Source: World Bank elaboration with a balanced panel from Orbis. No entry and exit dynamics considered for the analysis due to lack of data.

FIGURE 2.9

Access to credit, customs services, and red tape seem to have significant and large effects on TFP

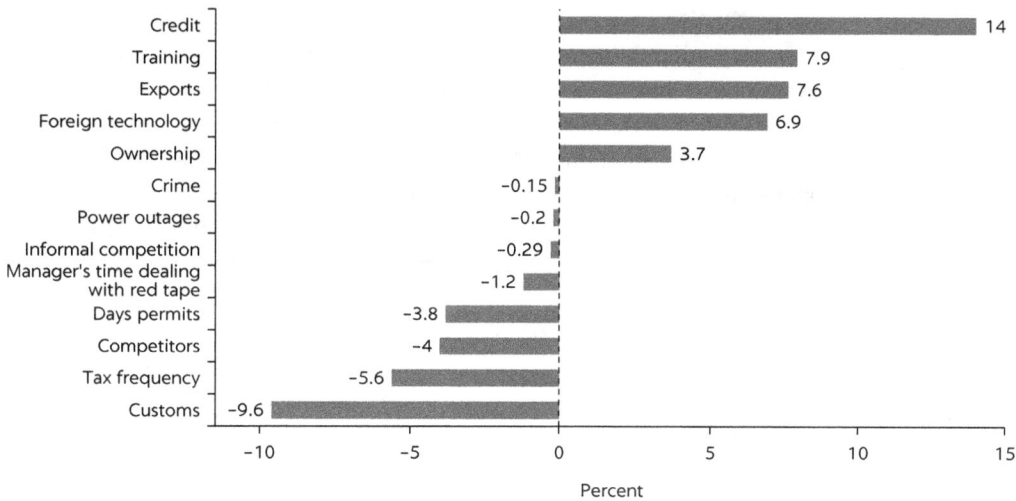

Credit — 14
Training — 7.9
Exports — 7.6
Foreign technology — 6.9
Ownership — 3.7
Crime — −0.15
Power outages — −0.2
Informal competition — −0.29
Manager's time dealing with red tape — −1.2
Days permits — −3.8
Competitors — −4
Tax frequency — −5.6
Customs — −9.6

Percent

Source: Productivity Background Note based on World Bank Enterprise Surveys, Romania 2013.
Note: The graph shows marginal effects of business environment and firm attribute variables on TFP.

Access to credit, customs services, and red tape seem to affect productivity performance. When estimating the marginal effects of the business environment and firm-level characteristics on TFP, access to credit appears to have the largest positive impact, by raising firms' TFP by 14 percent (compared with firms without access to credit). The positive effects of providing labor training and having access to foreign technology are within the 6–8 percent range. Meanwhile, red tape and regulation factors—managers' time spent with red tape, days to get a permit, times to clear exports in customs, and frequency of tax inspections—hold back TFP growth, highlighting how the institutional inefficiencies discussed in Chapter 5 can directly affect economic performance. The largest impact, however, comes from the time required to clear direct exports in customs, with one additional day reducing TFP by almost 10 percent (figure 2.9).[16]

Start-ups, as well as micro and small and medium enterprises (MSMEs), especially in rural areas, are not sufficiently served by the banking sector. With 23 enterprises per 1,000 people, Romania's business density is 56 percent lower than the rest of the EU. Of the 460,000 enterprises operating in industry and services, 88.5 percent are microenterprises, 11.1 percent are SMEs, and 0.4 percent are large firms.[17] Of these, only 128,000 companies are considered by banks to meet the minimum financial criteria for lending, suggesting tight credit for smaller enterprises. Start-ups do not have access to bank financing, as they lack track records and strong balance sheets to be used as collateral. Microenterprises tend to have informal practices and poor financial conditions (96.5 percent have negative equity, compared with 42.3 percent for all active enterprises). SMEs are a very heterogeneous group, with varied access to bank financing, although banks focus on urban areas, especially Bucharest, which accounts for more than a third of SME loans on average. Overall, banks compete to serve large firms, while foreign-owned firms, which account for 5.9 percent of total enterprises and 44 percent of total value added in 2015, tend to benefit from parent companies' centralized treasuries, which often borrow from banks or bond markets outside of Romania at a lower cost than the local subsidiaries can, making them more productive.

The unpredictability of the business environment, a direct consequence of institutional failures, is a significant challenge to business operations, including investment decisions. While a static analysis of the business regulatory environment does not portray a negative picture (Romania is ranked 45th in *Doing Business*), over the past years businesses were faced with a number of fiscal measures introduced and reversed, which severely impacted their ability to plan operations, including investments. While constraints to businesses activity vary depending on firm size, the unpredictability of the regulatory framework—in particular regarding taxation—is a concern for most enterprises. As mentioned in Chapter 5, the high number of changes to the fiscal code (20 changes in the last 2 years only), the lack of consultation with the private sector, and the short time given to businesses to adapt lead to delays in investment decisions. Because of their size and scarce MSMEs tend to be more affected by the regulatory burden. According to the EIB investment survey 2016, "political and regulatory climate" was the top factor negatively impacting firms' ability to carry out planned investment for 47 percent of Romanian firms, lower than in Poland (50 percent), but substantially higher than in other countries in the region, such as Bulgaria (17 percent), Hungary (23 percent), or Croatia (28 percent).

State control and barriers to entrepreneurship restrict product market competition and hold back productivity. Pro-competition regulation can help boost income per capita by increasing investment and employment, and it can also stimulate firms to become more innovative and efficient—thereby lifting aggregate productivity.[18] According to the Product Market Regulation (PMR) indicators, Romanian markets are characterized by higher levels of restrictiveness than comparator newer EU member countries. With a score of 1.69 out of 6, Romania's regulatory environment is more restrictive of competition than both the average EU country and regional peers, such as Bulgaria, Hungary, or Poland. A decomposition of the economy-wide PMR score shows that the restrictiveness of Romania's regulatory environment is driven by state control (55 percent) and barriers to entrepreneurship (41 percent), while Romania does well in terms of the barriers to trade and investment (4 percent). This reflects the widespread presence of SOEs in the economy and the direct involvement of the state in network services. At the same time, Romania could further lower barriers to entrepreneurship by enhancing the efficiency of the licenses and permits system and reducing administrative burdens on start-ups (figure 2.10).[19]

State control is apparent in the preeminence of SOEs in key sectors. With approximately 1,400 operational SOEs, of which about 200 are majority-controlled by the central government, Romania's SOE sector is the largest in the EU in terms of number of companies. As discussed in Chapter 5, poor corporate governance of SOEs leads to vast inefficiencies, with some companies generating large losses and SOEs receiving approximately 2 percent of total government spending (figure 2.11). SOEs in energy, gas, postal services, and transport are the most inefficient. Particularly in energy and gas, deregulation and a stable legal framework could boost competition and investments (including cross-border) and ensure sustainable and cost-efficient supply.

FIGURE 2.10

State control and barriers to entrepreneurship are the largest contributors to Romania's product market restrictions

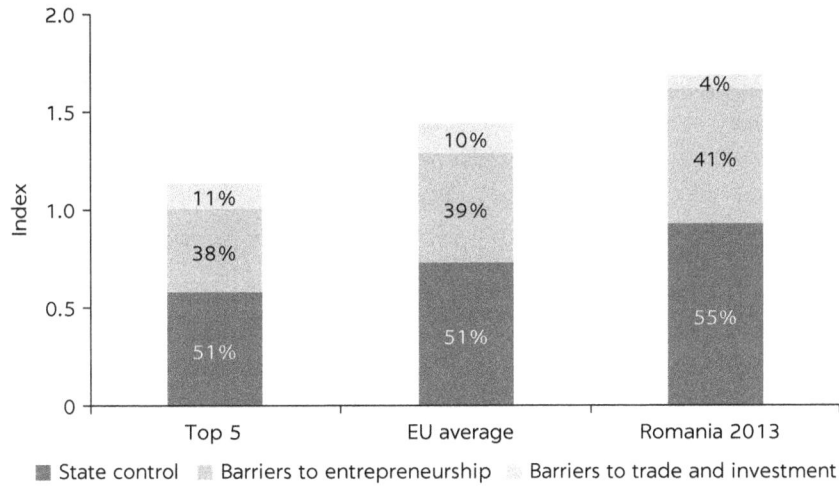

■ State control ▦ Barriers to entrepreneurship ▨ Barriers to trade and investment

Source: WBG-OECD Product Market Regulation data 2013–14.
Note: Index ranges between 0 and 6, from least to most restrictive.

FIGURE 2.11

Often inefficient SOEs are present in key sectors

a. Importance of SOEs in the economy

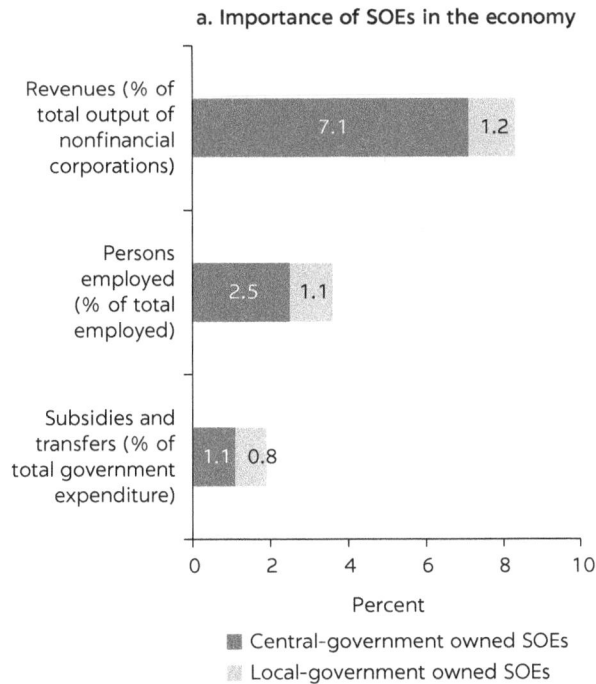

■ Central-government owned SOEs
▦ Local-government owned SOEs

Source: Ministry of Public Finance and European Commission.

b. Importance of SOEs by sector

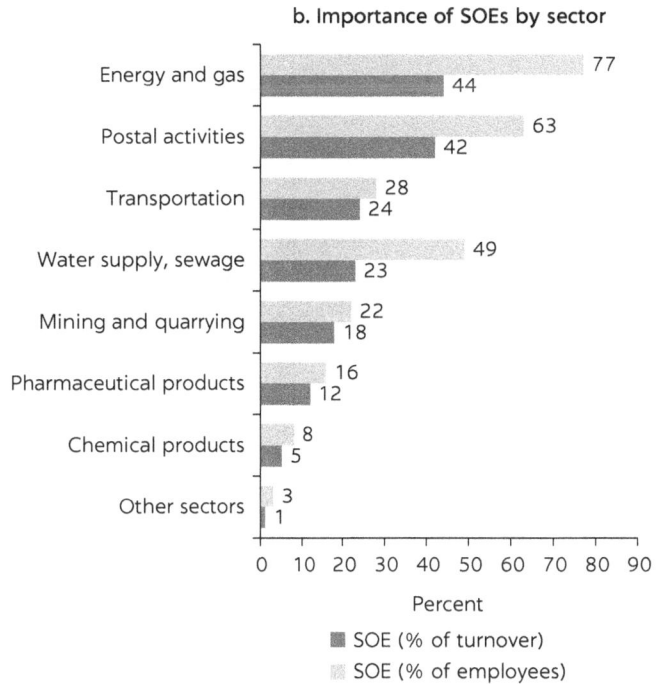

■ SOE (% of turnover)
▦ SOE (% of employees)

Source: Ministry of Public Finance and European Commission.

State aid is directed to declining industries, worsening the misallocation of resources. Consistently over time, the poorly performing railways sector has absorbed a sizeable portion of the overall state aid: 37.5 percent on average per year in 2010–2015.[20] Conversely, the state aid allocation for Research and Development or risk capital for MSMEs—areas that have the potential to spark growth— has been limited.[21] This introduces economic distortions that affect competition and induce resource misallocation toward less productive firms, negatively affecting aggregate productivity, both directly from low productivity firms and SOEs themselves, and indirectly through the inefficient supply of inputs to other sectors.

Restrictive regulation of services further constrains aggregate productivity. Reducing barriers in service sectors can increase productivity in the EU as a whole by an average of 5 percent, provide more and better jobs, stimulate investment, and encourage deeper integration (World Bank 2016). The service sector in Romania employs more than 50 percent of the workforce and accounts for more than 60 percent of GDP. A more competitive service sector can therefore significantly contribute to aggregate productivity. Although competition in services is in a relatively nascent phase in the EU, Romania stands out for particularly restrictive regulation of professional, transport, and airline services.

TAKING FULL ADVANTAGE OF THE EU SINGLE MARKET: TRADE AND INNOVATION

Romania successfully diversified its export basket toward medium-technology products, although the transformation slowed down after the Global Recession. Over the last two decades, Romania switched from labor-intensive

FIGURE 2.12

Romania's exports have become more technology intensive

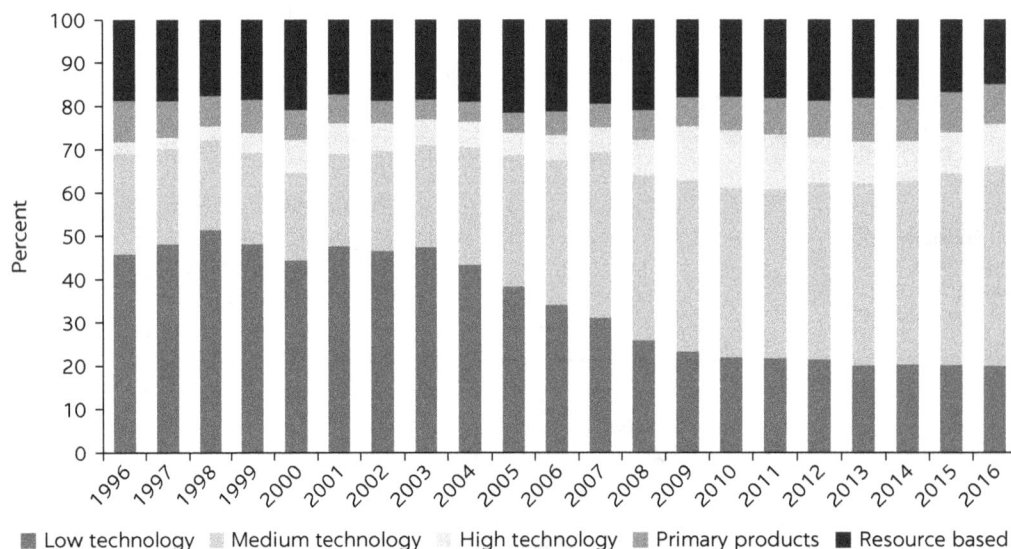

Source: United Nations International Trade Statistics Database (UN COMTRADE).

low-technology sectors, such as garments and footwear and metals, to more advanced sectors like automotive and machinery and electronic equipment (World Bank 2018e and box 2.2). However, this structural transformation slowed down after the financial crisis of 2008–2009. Overall, Romania

Product fitness of Romania's exports

Rapid increases in wealth have been accompanied by some improvement in Romania's capability stock (figure B2.2.1). These improvements present themselves as fitness gains in sectors including plastics, electrical equipment, and electronics (figure B2.2.2). Overall, Romania's per capita GDP is still lower than what is expected given its level of fitness, suggesting potential for Romania to continue its growth by fully utilizing its available endowments. With further diversification and an upgrade of its

capabilities, Romania can follow the pathway of countries like Hungary or South Korea. A range of industries present opportunities for Romania to achieve such capability development, including goods in very complex sectors such as machinery, chemicals, metal processing, and transportation equipment. Because of this broad sector fitness, Romania also has diversification opportunities in less complex industries, including crops, textiles, and animal products.

FIGURE B2.2.1

Product fitness and GDP per capita: growth trajectory

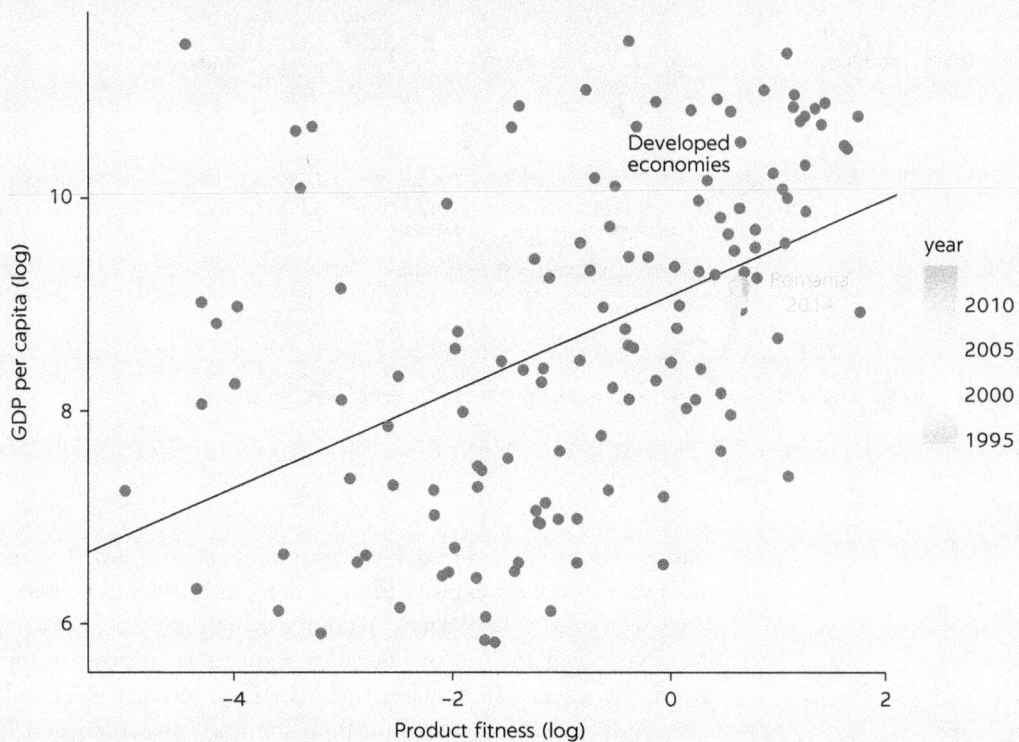

(continued)

BOX 2.2, *continued*

FIGURE B2.2.2

Romania's fitness rank by sector

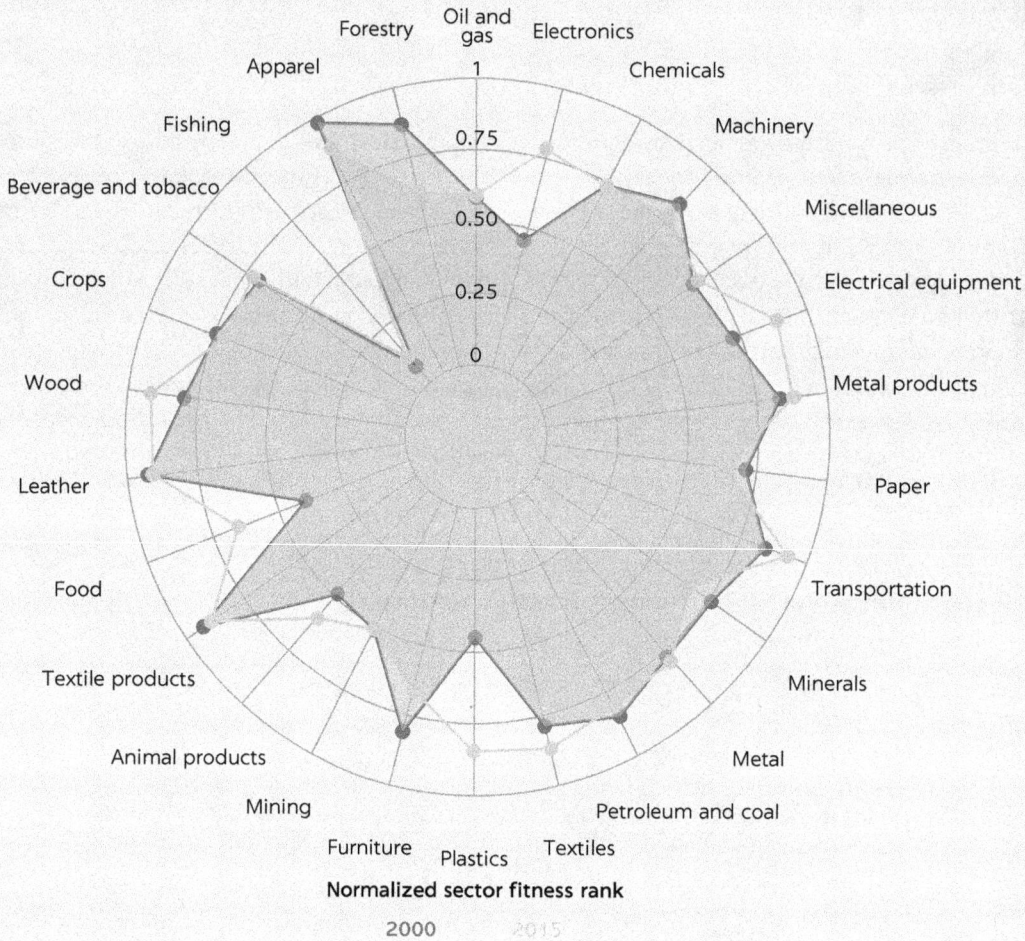

Normalized sector fitness rank

2000   2015

Sources: United Nations International Trade Statistics Database (UN COMTRADE), Country Opportunity Spotlight.

managed to improve the sophistication of its export basket by increasing its medium technology exports from 23 percent in 1996 to 46 percent in 2016. High-tech exports have accounted for less than 10 percent of total exports in every year over the last two decades. Exports from three of the main high technology exports in Romania (medicinal and pharma, electrical machinery and appliances, and scientific instruments) have recorded low quality increases (3.6 percent, 1.9 percent, and 1 percent respectively) between 1996 and 2010 that fall short of the quality increase of the automotive sector (8.8 percent), and are more in line with the quality performance of declining sectors like clothing and footwear. Furthermore, high technology exports exhibit the lowest survival probabilities in Romania, with less than 10 percent of export relationships surviving more than 5 years.

After 2008 export growth has increasingly been driven by existing products and markets. After 2008–2009, export growth relied more on the intensive margin (that is, exports of the same products to the same markets) compared with the preceding decade in which the extensive margin (that is, exports of new products or to new markets) accounted for almost half of export growth. The contribution of new export products to total export growth has declined from 44.5 percent in 1996–2008 to 4.7 percent in 2008–2016.

While benefiting from access to the EU market, Romanian firms are less integrated in global value chains (GVCs) than their regional peers, and tend to specialize in low-value-added activities. Thanks to EU membership, Romania's economy is open, with 75.8 percent of exports in 2017 going to the rest of the EU. However, more than 99 percent of Romanian firms are MSMEs, and only 25 percent of them export to other EU countries. Even exporters are not very innovative, and tend to specialize in assembly, low-value-added and downstream labor-intensive segments of GVCs, limiting opportunities to increase productivity.

Romania is classified by the EU Innovation Scoreboard as a modest innovator, limiting the ability of its firms to move up the value chain. Romanian firms underperform their EU peers in product and process innovation, marketing and organization innovation, research and development (R&D) innovation expenditure, patent applications, and ICT training. In 2016, the percentage of MSMEs introducing product or process innovations, marketing or organizational innovations, innovating in-house, or providing ICT training to their staff were well below EU levels, standing respectively at 4.9 percent, 8.8 percent, 4.5 percent, and 5 percent (figure 2.13). Also, Romania spends only about 0.5 percent GDP in R&D (of which only 43 percent is from the private sector) while the EU average is 2.03 percent GDP (figure 2.13). Patent applications, reflecting the capacity to exploit knowledge and translate it into economic gains, are also very low. In 2014, Romania's number of patent applications to the European Patent Office (EPO) was only 5.11

FIGURE 2.13

Romania's firms are not very innovative

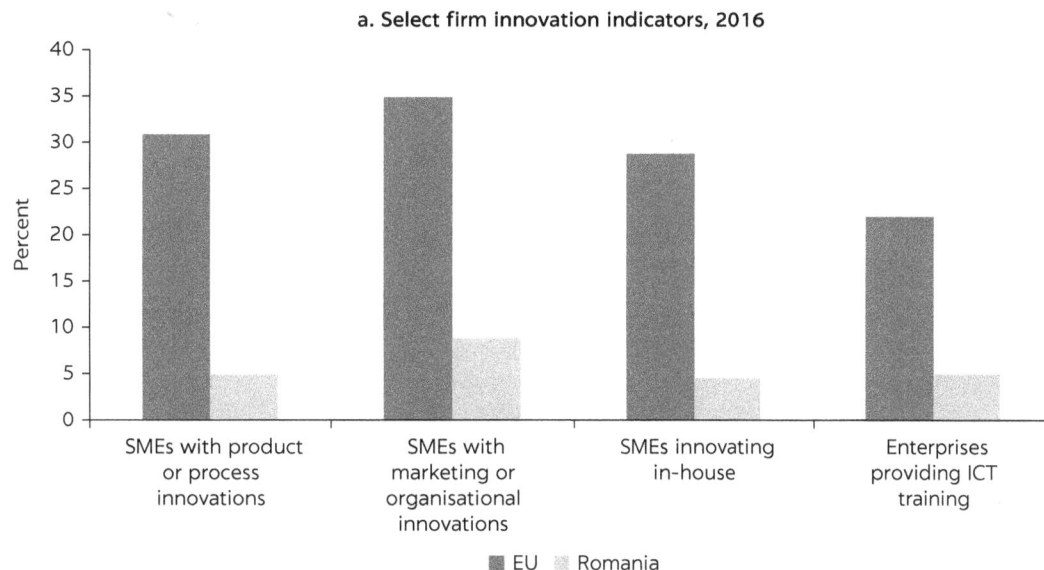

a. Select firm innovation indicators, 2016

Note: SMEs = small and medium enterprises; ICT = information and communications technology.

b. Patents application to the European Patent Office per million population, 2014

c. R&D expenditures by sector, 2015

■ Business enterprise ░ Higher education ░ Government

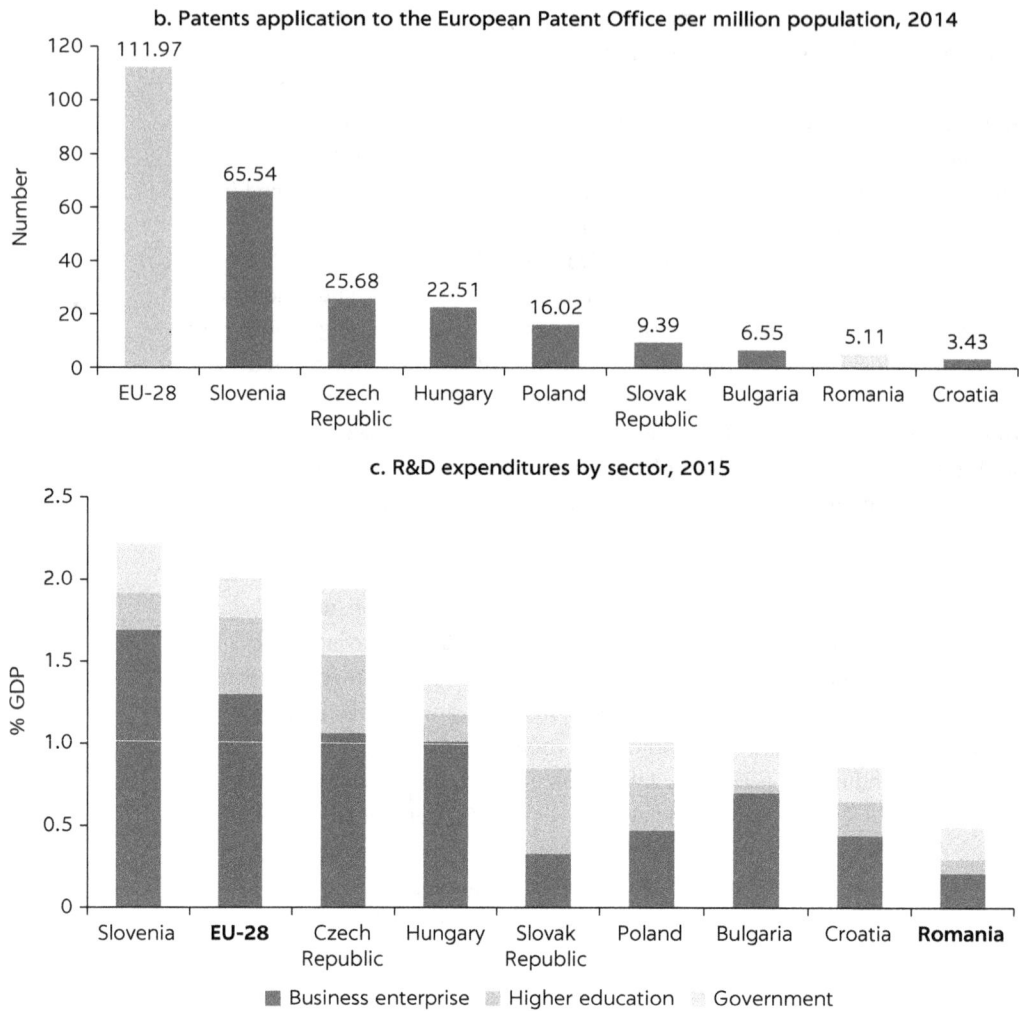

Sources: European Innovation Scoreboard 2017 and Eurostat.

per million people, 22 times lower than the EU average (figure 2.13). Innovation finance is also limited, with business angels almost nonexistent and venture capital amounting to .001 percent of GDP, well below the EU average of .027 percent.

NOTES

1. See World Bank (2018a and 2018c).
2. United Nations Population Division estimates the total number of Romanian emigrants at 3.4 million. Calculations based on Eurostat and national census data from the United States, Canada, Israel, and Ukraine, which are the top non-European countries in terms of the number of Romanian migrants, indicate a higher figure of just above 4 million.
3. According to UN (2017) *International Migration Report 2017*, the net migration outflow between 2000 and 2017 was about 2.44 million (calculated as the difference between the migration stock in 2017 and 2000).
4. STEM = Sciences, Technologies, Engineering, and Mathematics.
5. In 2016 VET accounted for only 1 percent of total public expenditures on education.
6. World Bank's 2017 Online Employer Survey (World Bank 2018a).
7. The Romanian economy is particularly vulnerable to this trend, as it currently has a disproportionate share of these types of jobs in the manufacturing, IT, and agriculture sectors.

8. The literature suggests that upwards of 60 percent of all jobs will be replaced by machines over the coming two decades. See: Acemoglu, D., and P. Restrepo. 2016.

9. After Romania, the second-lowest banking assets to GDP ratio is 88.1 percent for Slovenia, and the highest is 128 percent for Czech Republic.

10. http://newfinancial.eu/report-the-size-depth-growth-opportunity-in-eu-capital -markets/

11. The Bucharest Stock Exchange is in the process of attaining Emerging Market status (from Frontier Market) and the Romanian capital market is considered to have substantial potential to be upgraded to the same. Once this status is reached, Romania could be included in MSCI EM indices, which would have a significant impact on investment inflows. It is estimated that these additional inflows could reach US$1.3 billion (including mutual funds, exchange-traded funds and institutional funds). Potential privatizations would represent important steps for achieving Emerging Market status, and unleash the potential of international investments.

12. Higher FDI inflows during this period were driven by intensification of the privatization process.

13. https://ec.europa.eu/transport/facts-fundings/scoreboard/compare/energy-union-inno vation/share-electrified-railway_en

14. https://cohesiondata.ec.europa.eu/countries/RO

15. For productivity analysis based on Orbis firm level data, see World Bank (2018b).

16. For more details on the methodology used, see Correa, Cusolito and Pena (2017).

17. As of December 31, 2015. Data from EUROSTAT.

18. On the impact of services sector reforms on productivity, see World Bank (2016a).

19. Recent changes in the regulatory framework, including the deregulation of electricity prices in 2017 and efforts to lower business registration costs, might have reduced the restrictiveness of Romania's Product Market Regulation compared to 2013.

20. See http://ec.europa.eu/competition/state_aid/scoreboard/technical_note_en.pdf.

21. State support for entrepreneurship and the private sector is fragmented across different institutions and programs, often not administered in an efficient and sustainable manner. Programs are spread out among 17 different entities, leading to inefficient management of resources, weak monitoring, and limited impact. No impact evaluation has been carried out.

REFERENCES

Acemoglu, D., and P. Restrepo. 2016. "The Race between Machine and Man: Implications of Technology for Growth, Factor Shares and Employment." Working Paper No. 22252, National Bureau of Economic Research, Cambridge, MA.

Correa, P., Ana P. Cusolito and J. Pena. 2017. "What Firm-Level Data Say about the Effects of the Business Environment on Productivity." Background Paper for the forthcoming World Bank Global Productivity flagship report.

OECD (Organisation for Economic Co-operation and Development). 2017. *G20 Global Displacement and Migration Trends Report 2017*. Paris: OECD Publishing.

OECD and UN–DESA (Organisation for Economic Co-operation and Development and United Nations Department of Economic and Social Affairs). 2013. *World Migration in Figures*. New York: United Nations.

World Bank. 2016. EU Regular Economic Report - Growth, Jobs and Integration: Services to the Rescue. Washington, DC: World Bank.

——. 2018a. Background Note for the Romania Systematic Country Diagnostic. Education.

——. 2018b. Background Note for the Romania Systematic Country Diagnostic. Productivity.

——. 2018c. Background Note for the Romania Systematic Country Diagnostic. Migration.

——. 2018d. Background Note for the Romania Systematic Country Diagnostic. Natural Capital.

——. 2018e. Background Note for the Romania Systematic Country Diagnostic. Trade.

3 Expanding Opportunities for Shared Prosperity

THE EU ACCESSION WAS A BOON, BUT GROWTH HAS NOT LED TO EQUITY

Today, Romania prospers—but prosperity is not shared equally, as the bottom 40 is largely disconnected from the drivers of growth. Manufacturing, trade, and ICT have been the main sectors driving economic growth in recent years; however, the benefits of growth do not flow to the bottom 40, given their limited access to productive jobs: close to half of the people in the bottom 40 percent of the income distribution do not work, and another 28 percent are engaged in subsistence agriculture (figure 3.1). As thriving sectors and labor markets broadly fail to lift marginalized and socially excluded groups out of poverty, the ones left behind remain detached from the prosperity generated by a handful of thriving urban centers that enjoy a living standard that is on par with Western Europe.

Romania's inclusion challenge is predominantly a rural problem, with 75 percent of the poor living in rural areas.[1] The incomplete structural transformation is associated with an uneven spatial distribution of opportunities, with 45 percent of the population still residing in rural areas where poverty is a full 20 percentage points higher than in urban areas. Disparities in living standards between urban and rural areas are striking: mean urban income is almost 50 percent higher than mean rural income, a gap that is the second-highest in the EU. Poor regions in Romania are also where most of the poor live: poverty is spatially concentrated in the North-East region, where the share of poor in some counties is more than ten times higher than that in Bucharest (map 3.1).

The transition to more productive jobs has been limited, as most of the employment growth in the last decade came from nontradable, low-end services, and increases in labor income were fragile. A large share of the employment growth prior to the crisis occurred in construction and real estate activities, and to a lesser extent in trade, driven by a rapid reallocation of labor from the rural

---

The diagnostic in this chapter is guided by the asset framework (Bussolo and Lopez-Calva 2014).

FIGURE 3.1

A large share of the bottom 40 does not work or relies on subsistence agriculture

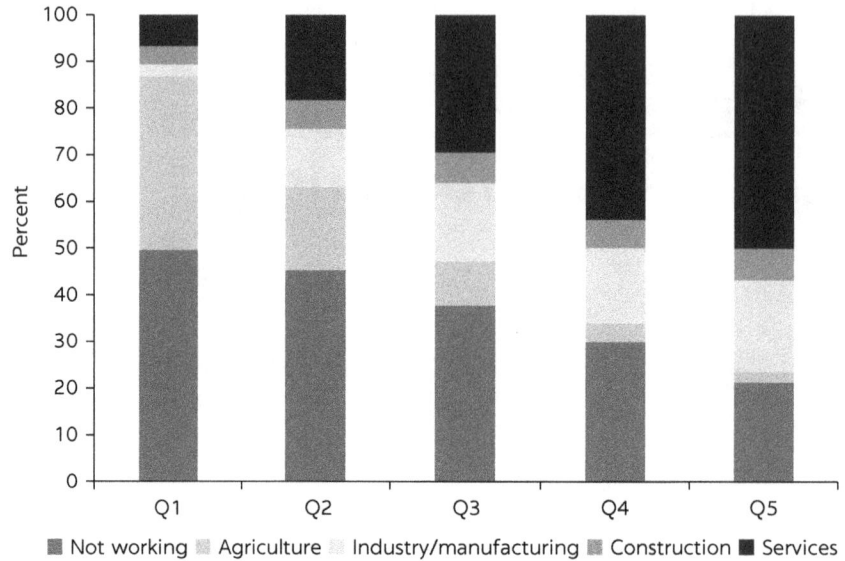

■ Not working ▦ Agriculture ░ Industry/manufacturing ▨ Construction ■ Services

Source: World Bank calculation using European Union Statistics on Income and Living Conditions (EU–SILC) 2016.
Note: Figure shows the sectoral employment distribution by income quintile, with Q1 indicating the bottom 20 percent.

MAP 3.1

Poor regions are where most of the poor live

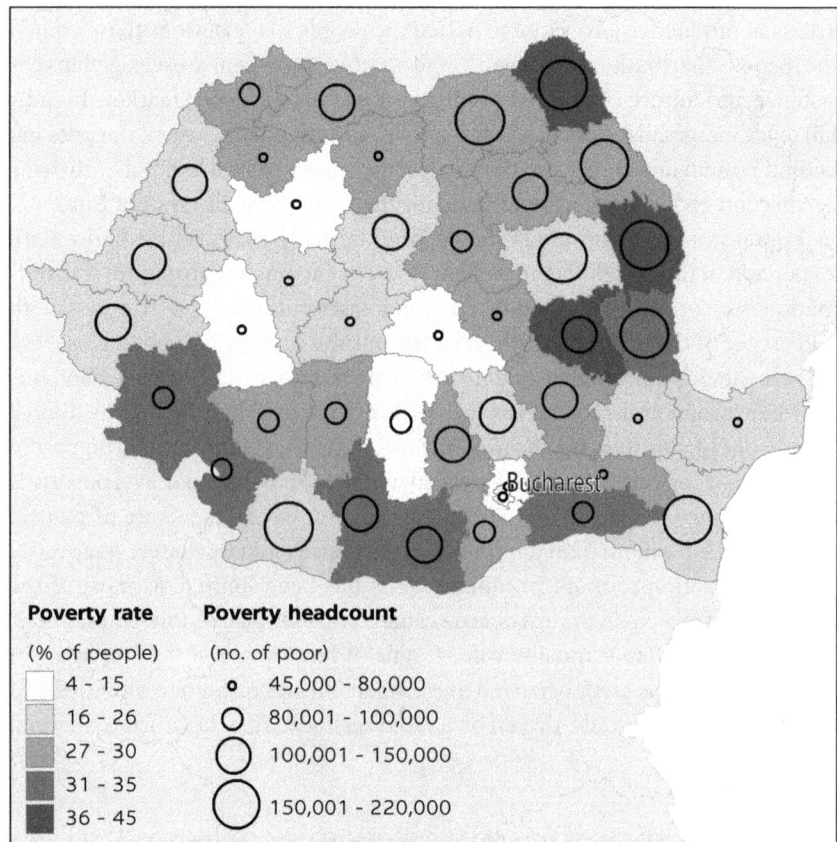

Poverty rate

(% of people)

- 4 - 15
- 16 - 26
- 27 - 30
- 31 - 35
- 36 - 45

Poverty headcount

(no. of poor)

- 45,000 - 80,000
- 80,001 - 100,000
- 100,001 - 150,000
- 150,001 - 220,000

Source: World Bank illustration based on World Bank (2016).

FIGURE 3.2

Large labor movements occurred between the agricultural sector and low-end services

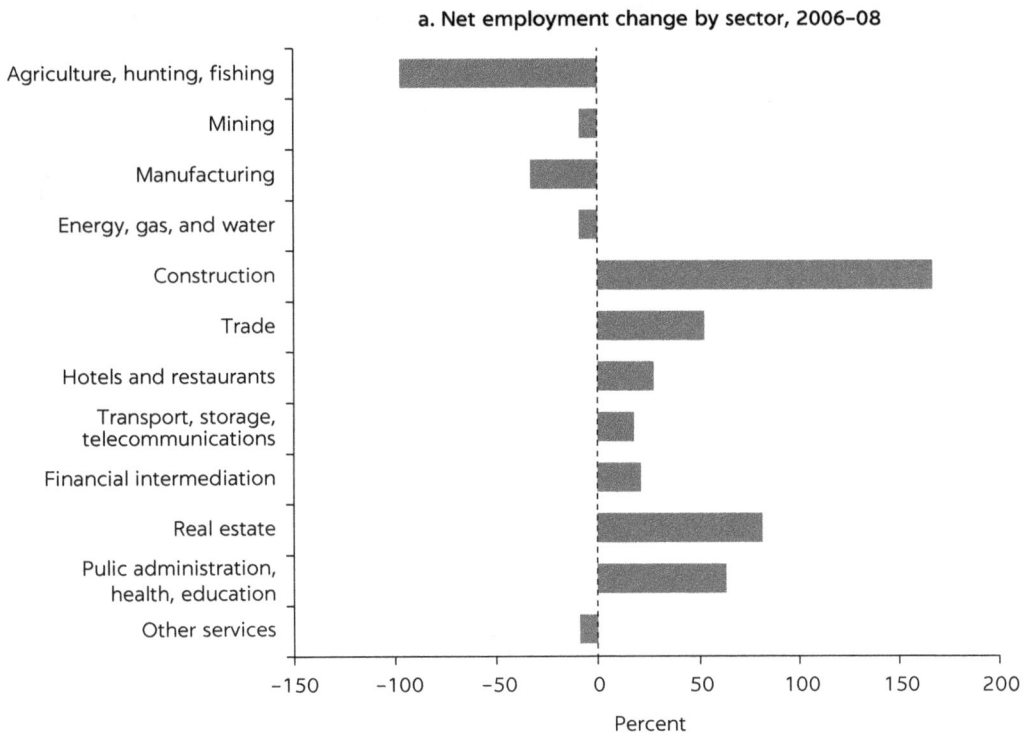

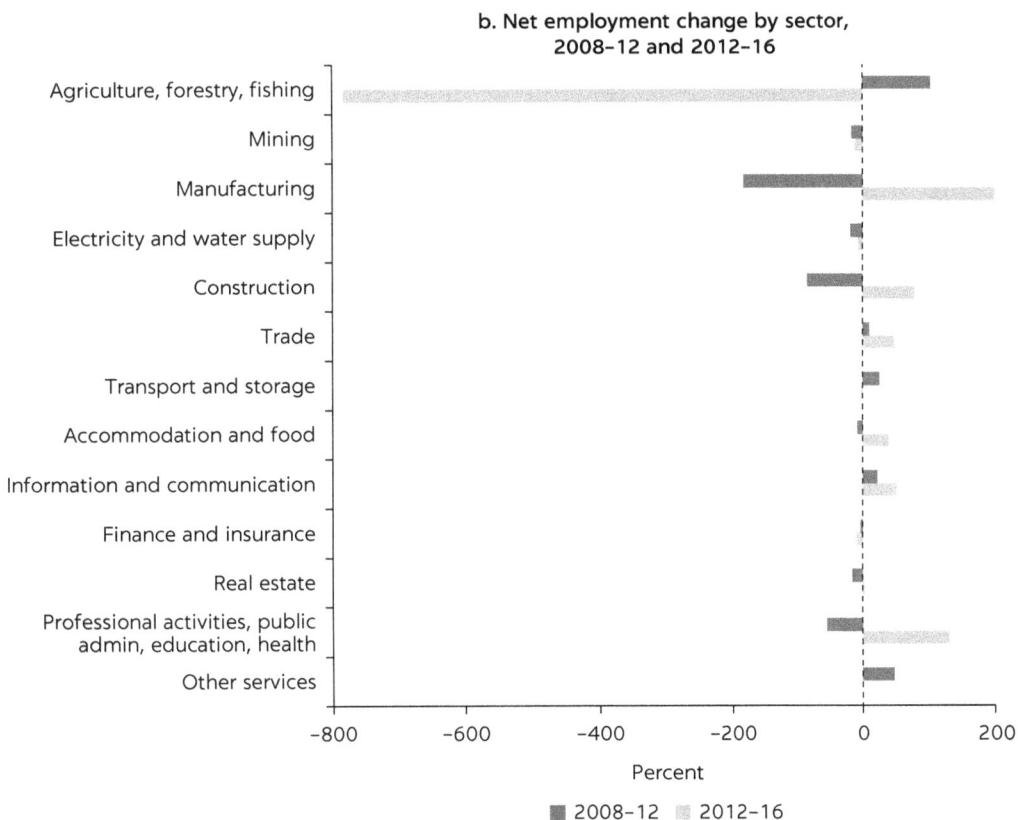

a. Net employment change by sector, 2006–08

b. Net employment change by sector, 2008–12 and 2012–16

■ 2008–12   ▨ 2012–16

Source: National Institute Statistics.
Note: Note different scales. The classification of sector of activity is based on the Classification of Activities from National Economy (CANE) rev. 1 until 2008 and CANE rev. 2 after 2008. Some small sectors are aggregated for better comparison.

FIGURE 3.3

Prosperity was shared before the financial crisis, but incomes of the bottom 40 have been slow to recover postcrisis

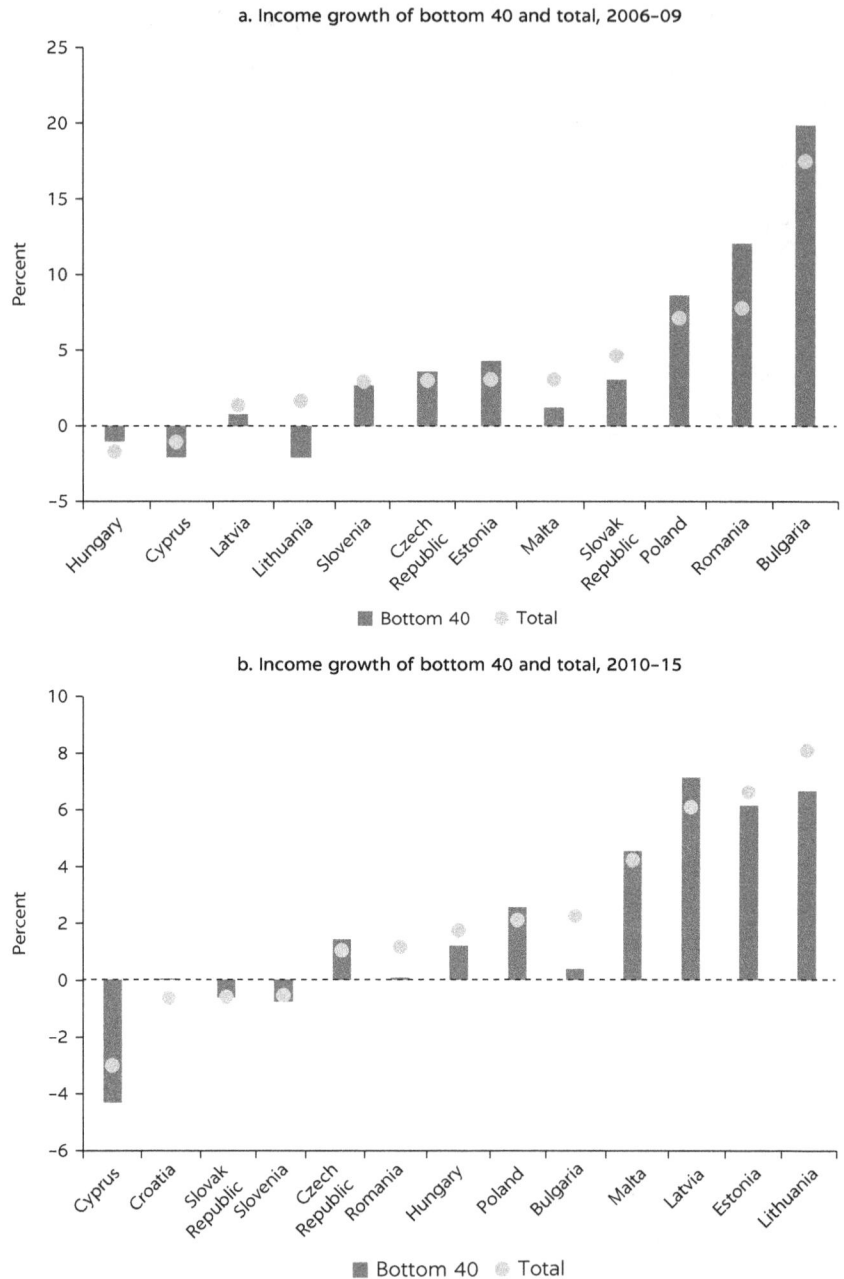

a. Income growth of bottom 40 and total, 2006–09

■ Bottom 40　　● Total

b. Income growth of bottom 40 and total, 2010–15

■ Bottom 40　　● Total

Source: World Bank calculation using EU-Statistics on Income and Living Conditions (EU-SILC).

agricultural sector (figure 3.2a). This led to broad-based wage growth and contributed to the positive shared prosperity premium between 2006 and 2009 (figure 3.3a).[2] While labor market improvements did contribute to poverty reduction, pensions were the main drivers of poverty reduction during this period (figure 3.4). Moreover, while these low-skilled sectors pay better and employ a disproportionately large share of people in the bottom 40, they are demand-constrained and sensitive to business cycles. The consequences of this became evident with the arrival of the financial crisis, when these sectors shed a

FIGURE 3.4

Pensions helped a large number of people escape poverty before the crisis but could not be sustained after the crisis

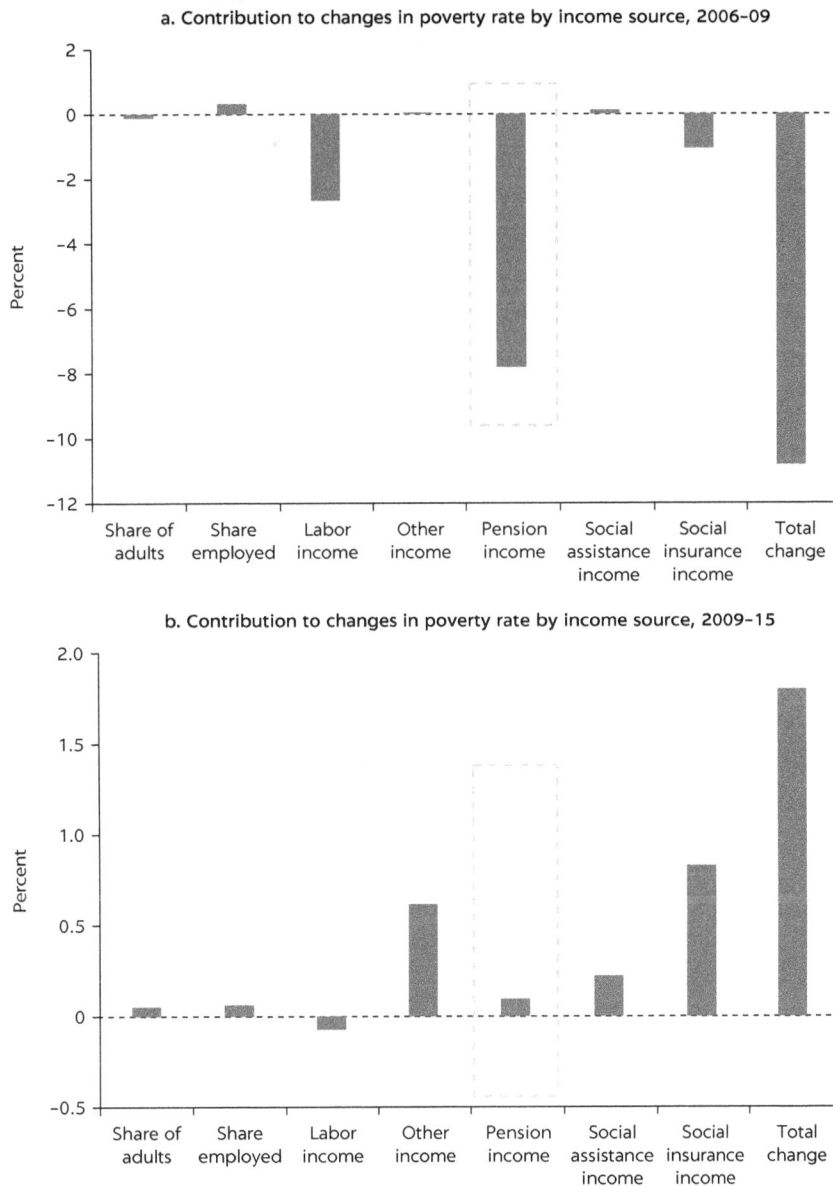

a. Contribution to changes in poverty rate by income source, 2006–09

b. Contribution to changes in poverty rate by income source, 2009–15

Source: World Bank calculation using EU-Statistics on Income and Living Conditions (EU-SILC).
Note: Figures show the marginal contribution to change in poverty rate in percentage points by source of income. Note different scales.

large number of jobs. Low-skilled people fell back on agricultural activities (figure 3.2b) and the incomes of the bottom 40 were hit particularly hard (figure 3.3b). The lesson from this experience is that constraints to equal opportunities, and structural factors that limit transitions to more productive jobs and labor market dynamism, need to be addressed for labor markets to successfully and sustainably contribute to poverty reduction and shared prosperity.

The strong duality observed in Romania is a manifestation of unequal opportunities and unequal access to markets that has no parallel in any other EU country. Weak institutions are the common denominator. Education is one of the most important predictors of poverty: people with only primary education are

FIGURE 3.5

Poverty is substantially higher for people with primary or less education, and for rural populations

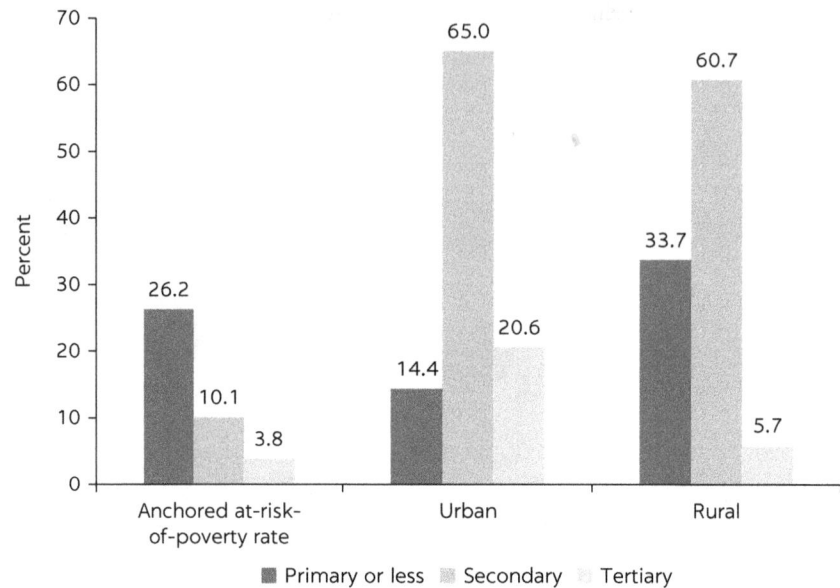

Source: World Bank estimation using EU-Statistics on Income and Living Conditions (EU-SILC) 2015 (L); Household Budget Survey 2016 (R).
Note: Figure shows anchored AROP rates by education, and educational attainment by urban and rural populations. AROP = at risk of poverty.

significantly more likely to be poor than people with tertiary education (figure 3.5). However, the rural labor force remains highly unskilled: a third of working-age adults in rural areas have only completed primary education or less. There are few productive opportunities in rural areas, partly because physical connectivity with urban areas is lacking. Informal property rights are significantly more prevalent in rural areas, which affect land development, investment, scaling-up of production, and thus the returns to factors of production. The gap in access to public services—potable water, sanitation, energy—is predominantly from low coverage in rural areas. Uneven endowments and structural factors that influence the returns to endowments together shape the marked divide observed across social groups and locations. Finally, fiscal policies have failed to counter high levels of inequality, because an increasingly large share of the poor is not entitled to pensions, and social assistance is not well-targeted. Low internal mobility implies that the rural population falls increasingly behind. Functional challenges of the government that include corruption, weak commitment to policy implementation, weak local service delivery, and an inability to ensure sufficient local funding as a result of patronage-based politics have led to slow progress across the spectrum. The following sections lay out an in-depth diagnostic of the constraints that led to the lack of shared prosperity and the two Romanias.

EQUAL OPPORTUNITIES ARE THE BEDROCK OF EQUITY POLICIES, BUT THEY ALSO MATTER FOR GROWTH

Closing the human capital gap is a precondition for sustainable poverty reduction, but progress has been limited. Large gaps in education and health lead to unequal opportunities for the poor, and especially the Roma population, holding up the transition to more productive jobs. Educational outcomes are lagging, especially in rural areas where the rate of early school leaving, at 27 percent, is alarmingly high. Program for International Student Assessment (PISA) scores show that about 40 percent of Romanian 15-year-old students are functionally innumerate and illiterate, with students from rural areas and disadvantaged backgrounds more likely to underperform. There are significant differences in PISA performance among students from the top and bottom socioeconomic quintiles, equivalent to three years of schooling in PISA 2015. Social school segregation has been increasing over the years, with poorer students attending lower-quality schools. As a consequence, only 1 percent of high-performing schools and about 83 percent of low performing schools are in rural areas, and are generally unable to attract and retain full-time qualified staff (OECD 2016; World Bank 2018b). The issue of school segregation is worse for Roma children, as almost a third of them are educated in segregated schools with a majority of Roma students, leading to even wider gaps in the quality of education and reinforcing patterns of segregation (World Bank 2014b).

Early childhood education has been shown to provide the foundation of cognitive and socio-emotional skills, yet coverage remains very low nationally for children under the age of 3. Early years' services are often not accessible to the most disadvantaged children and families. While the net preschool enrollment rate has steadily increased over the last ten years—from 72 percent in 2005 to 87.6 percent in 2015—it is still below the EU average of 94.8 percent. Moreover, only 38 percent of Roma children attend early childhood education and care, and the situation has worsened since 2011, when the figure was 45 percent (European Union Agency for Fundamental Rights 2016).

The health care system is a social health insurance system that is in principle compulsory, but in practice covers only about 86 percent of the population. Notably excluded are agricultural workers, the Roma who lack identity cards, the informally employed, and the unemployed or self-employed who are not registered for unemployment or social security benefits.[3] The insured are entitled to a comprehensive benefits package, while the uninsured receive minimum benefits.[4]

The health system is overregulated, which leads to a complicated administration and funding system, creating barriers in access of health services. The development of the public health sector with a comprehensive and integrated services network remains a challenge. The public hospital sector is large and fragmented, and there is a need to reconfigure existing hospitals to long-term or rehabilitation care. The coverage of the health facility network is sparse in rural areas, where resources are even more limited and distances far.

Low access to quality care for all, but especially for the poor, is the consequence of a weak primary care system and lack of continuity of care (World Bank 2018d). Cervical cancer has an excellent prognosis for cure if detected and treated early, but low screening rates for Romanian women lead to one of the highest mortality rates in the region. Yet another indication of a poorly performing health system is the deteriorating vaccination rates for diphtheria-tetanus-pertussis and poliomyelitis, which were 99 percent in 2000 but dropped to less than 90 percent in 2013 (WHO 2016). Disparities in access to care, combined with the influence of socioeconomic factors, lead to a wide socioeconomic gradient in health outcomes. For example, infant mortality is 60 percent higher in rural areas than in urban areas, and the incidence of hypertension is more than double among the low-educated people compared with the high-educated. High out-of-pocket payments exacerbate gaps in access to health care, as unmet needs are high among the poor and vulnerable. This particularly impacts the management of noncommunicable diseases. Disparities in access to health care services are high: 13.2 percent of the adult population in the bottom income quintile reported having unmet health care needs, compared with only 4.8 percent in the top quintile.[5]

Institutional capacity shapes the quality and equity of human capital formation, but a lack of commitment to long-term policies and underfunding are at the core of slow and uneven progress. Key national strategies have been put in place to improve education and health services, but progress has been slow and insufficient to help Romania confront the imminent consequences of a rapidly declining and aging population.[6] The biggest challenges are induced by frequent changes in policies: between 2005 and 2013, the Ministry of National Education and the Ministry of Health have seen a turnover of 33 and 16 ministers, respectively. The insufficient capacity of public policy units can lead to ad hoc decisions, as further discussed in Chapter 5. The lack of adequate monitoring and accountability lead to mismanagement and inefficient use of funds in the education sector. More efficient and transparent management of funds is needed, through strategic planning exercises linking policy to both national and EU resources (World Bank 2018b). In the health sector, low pay, inadequate working conditions, and frustrations with the current system lead to a shortage of health care professionals, which is further exacerbated by emigration and a culture of informal payments—the latter reinforcing unequal access to health care. Underfinancing is a persistent issue, as both education and health expenditures are among the lowest in the EU, at 3.7 percent and 4.0 percent of GDP respectively in 2016.

A focus on equal opportunities would transform the inclusive growth agenda into action and, looking ahead, would help mitigate the impact of technology on earnings disparities. Technological disruption and automation are widely predicted to accelerate the dispersion of incomes and opportunities. Between 1998 and 2013, the biggest shift in the skills content of jobs occurred toward routine cognitive tasks in Romania (figure 3.6). This stands out in comparison to other new EU member states where the largest shift occurred toward nonroutine cognitive tasks (Hardy, Keister and Lewandowski 2016). While this may reflect Romania's different occupational structure and supply as well as demand for labor, experience from other countries suggests that the direct effects of automation, including polarization of labor markets, will take effect in Romania in the near future.

Equalizing opportunities starting at early childhood, where the bulk of cognitive and socio-emotional skills are formed, will go a long way toward improving the skills distribution of the population and preventing a further widening of inequality because of new technology. This is especially relevant for the future generation: a popular estimate suggests that 65 percent of today's young children will be working in categories of jobs and functions that do not currently exist (World Economic Forum 2016).

Inclusive growth is jointly determined by the opportunities of people and firms to thrive and contribute productively to the economy, but Romania is currently underperforming in both dimensions (World Bank 2017b). As technology also creates more opportunities for entrepreneurship and the lines

FIGURE 3.6

Jobs have increasingly become intensive in cognitive tasks, 1998–2014

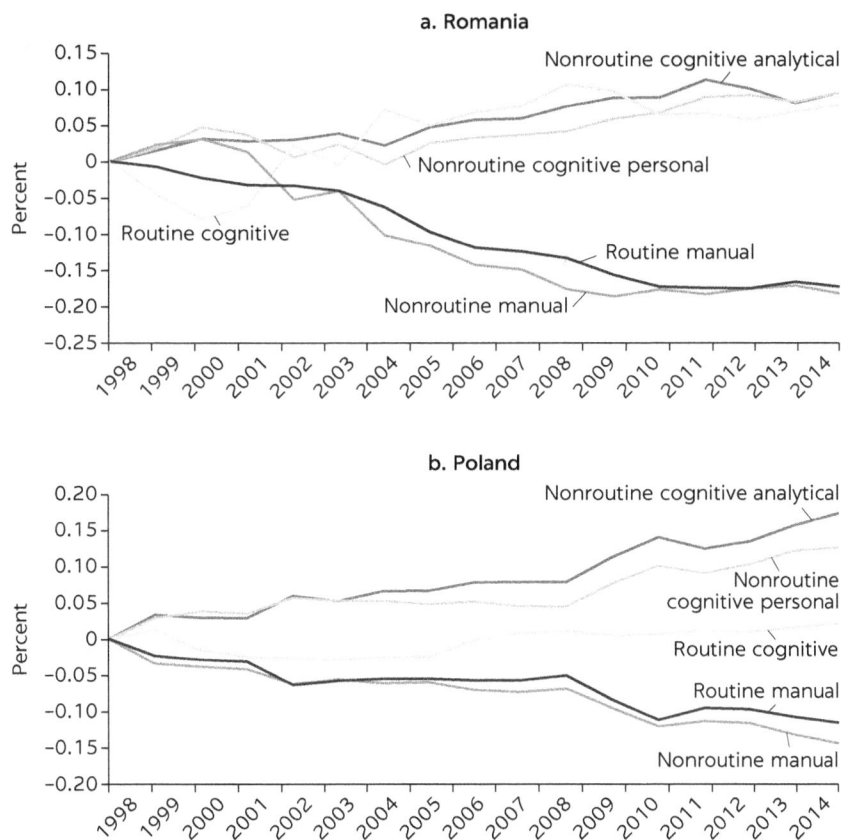

a. Romania

b. Poland

Source: Hardy, Keister, and Lewandowski 2016.

between people and firms disappear, the principle of equal opportunity can be extended to support both, where the success of neither is determined by circumstances of individuals at birth or by the lack of an enabling environment for firms. An enabling environment for firms is thus critical to inclusive growth in expanding employment, boosting wages, and widening asset ownership.

High inequality is associated with unequal opportunities; thus, inequality has a profound effect on children, which can impede economic mobility and the economy's long-run growth potential. Recent evidence supports a largely negative relationship between inequality and growth (OECD 2017; Grigoli and Robles 2017). Checchi, Peragine, and Serlenga (2016) suggest that a large share of income inequality can be traced back to unequal starts, especially in countries like Romania that spend less on education as a share of GDP, particularly at the preprimary level. International comparisons suggest that more inequality is associated with less economic mobility, as shown in the "Great Gatsby Curve" (figure 3.7).

Worryingly, Romania's mobility is already lower than its EU peers (table 3.1). In Romania, 44 percent of children with parents who have completed only

FIGURE 3.7

The Great Gatsby curve: more inequality, less mobility

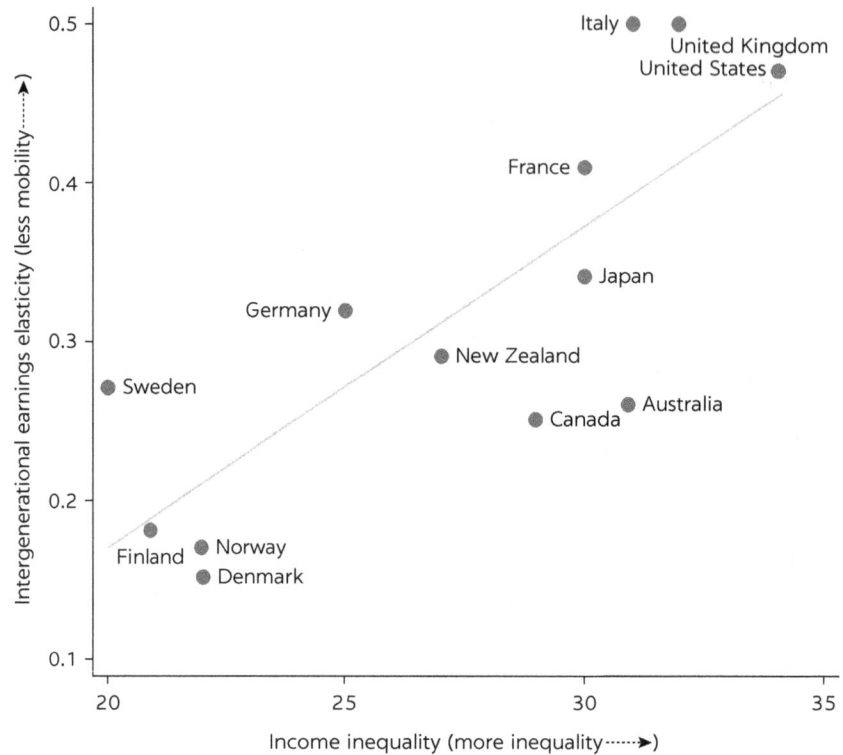

Source: Corak 2013.

primary education are not able to move up the education ladder. In Poland, more than 70 percent of children that start out in the same circumstances are able to achieve upper secondary education. Education is the most powerful engine of social mobility, but the participation of Roma children in early childhood education is less than half the national figure (FRA 2016). This translates into higher drop-out rates from primary and secondary schools, and a situation where being Roma increases the chances of poverty more than any other circumstantial factor.

Many children accumulate disadvantages that are the direct result of poverty and deprivation. About 4 out of 10 Romanian children are poor, the highest number in the EU. External migrants disproportionately originate from poorer regions, which leads to close to 100,000 children being left behind.[7] There is great concern about these children, yet little is known about the welfare consequences.[8] The few available studies suggest that these children exhibit lower subjective well-being, and strong negative impacts on health and education tend to be found when both parents are away. A more systematic effort and better data are needed to assess the welfare consequences on these children.

The Roma are among the most marginalized groups: a staggering 70 percent live in poverty, and spatial segregation and discrimination remain high. The Roma community is estimated to represent up to 12 percent of the population, yet being Roma is one of the worst social stigmas in Romania. As a result, 68 percent of Roma people live in majority Roma neighborhoods. Some progress has been made to improve the social and economic inclusion of Roma people, but

TABLE 3.1 **Educational mobility in Romania is low compared with peers**

ISCED LEVELS	CHILDREN		
	PRIMARY OR LESS	UPPER SECONDARY	TERTIARY
Parents	Poland		
Primary or less	21.7	71.5	6.7
Upper secondary	13.2	61.0	25.8
Tertiary	15.9	28.9	55.2
	Romania		
Primary or less	44.2	51.9	3.9
Upper secondary	17.5	60.6	21.8
Tertiary	14.6	27.4	58.0
	Bulgaria		
Primary or less	45.1	48.5	6.4
Upper secondary	8.4	64.0	27.6
Tertiary	11.1	34.7	54.2

Source: EUROSTAT.
Note: International Standard Classification of Education (ISCED) 2011 education levels, collapsed into primary (1), upper secondary (2), and tertiary (3) education completed.

there is a long way to go: only one in three Roma engages in paid work, and a third of Roma people live in households that experienced hunger in the previous month (FRA 2016). Early marriage and childbearing is much more common among Roma women, reinforcing dependency and further limiting their prospects.

The root cause of these disadvantages can be found early in life and in disparities accessing the most basic services: Romania has one of the highest shares of early school leavers in the EU, but the figure is almost four times higher for Roma, at 77 percent. Despite a universal health care system, only 54 percent of Roma are covered by health insurance. Meanwhile, 67 percent of Roma live in households without tap water, and 82 percent are without a toilet inside their dwellings, versus 38.1 percent and 31.2 percent, respectively, of those in the non-Roma population (FRA 2016; World Bank 2014b).

The issues of segregation, informal settlements, and basic infrastructure are intertwined. A third of Roma households did not receive land titles during the restitution process, which in some cases inhibits access to education and health services. Residing in informal settlements often precludes the legal construction of basic infrastructure (World Bank 2014b). There is a relatively strong political commitment to Roma inclusion at the national and EU level, as evidenced by the National Roma Integration Strategy (NRIS) 2015–2010, and substantial financing from state, local, and EU instruments. However, the contribution of this agenda remains to be seen in the form of concrete action and sustained commitment (World Bank 2018e).[9]

Significant efforts will be required to address the persistent exclusion faced by Roma, but the potential economic benefits of bringing Roma up to the standards of non-Roma employees could be substantial. Estimates suggest that Roma labor market inclusion could expand the economy by up to 3 percent of GDP annually, and bring about significant increases in fiscal revenues through tax contributions (World Bank 2010).

Concerted efforts are required to improve human capital services in lagging regions, with targeted interventions that reach marginalized groups and communities, and to improve integration with leading areas. Inequality of opportunities is underpinned by stark regional disparities and a deep urban–rural divide. Moreover, close to 5 percent of the population live in marginalized areas, characterized by low income, disproportionately low human capital, limited formal employment and inadequate housing conditions. A shift from a focus on convergence to maximizing regional economic potential and maintaining equity through equal opportunities may be more effective at achieving the goals under the EU Cohesion Policy to reduce economic, social, and territorial disparities. Raising human capital endowments and enhancing mobility through infrastructure investments can substantially increase the potential for productivity-enhancing agglomeration and provide a path to prosperity for lagging regions, without necessarily having to "balance growth."[10]

PROSPERITY CAN BE SHARED BY BOOSTING PRODUCTIVE EMPLOYMENT

Expanding access to earnings opportunities is essential given high poverty rates and declining demographic trends, but the employment rate has remained conspicuously stagnant. There is a pronounced and persistent employment gap between the working-age population in the poorest and top three quintiles: the gap is equivalent to 16 percentage points for men and 30 percentage points for women (figure 3.8). Despite quickly rising wages and wider labor shortages across the skills spectrum, employment rates have increased rather slowly, and remain at low levels. Employment growth has by and large been insensitive to cyclical fluctuations, and has only recently started to show signs of modest improvement (figure 3.9). The construction sector played an instrumental role in providing access to jobs for low-skilled workers before the crisis, but continued coordination challenges among government agencies and bottlenecks in EU funds absorption have led to very low investment in the transport sector (as further detailed in Chapter 5). This results in significant missed opportunities,

FIGURE 3.8

There is a large employment gap between top (1st) and bottom (3rd–5th) quintiles

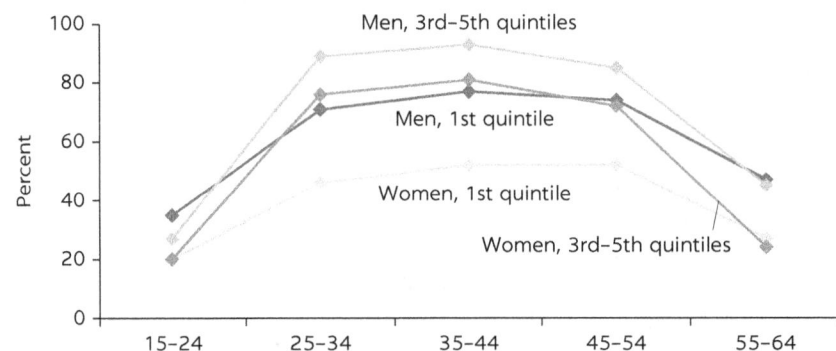

Source: World Bank 2015.

FIGURE 3.9

Romania's employment rate has been very slow to improve

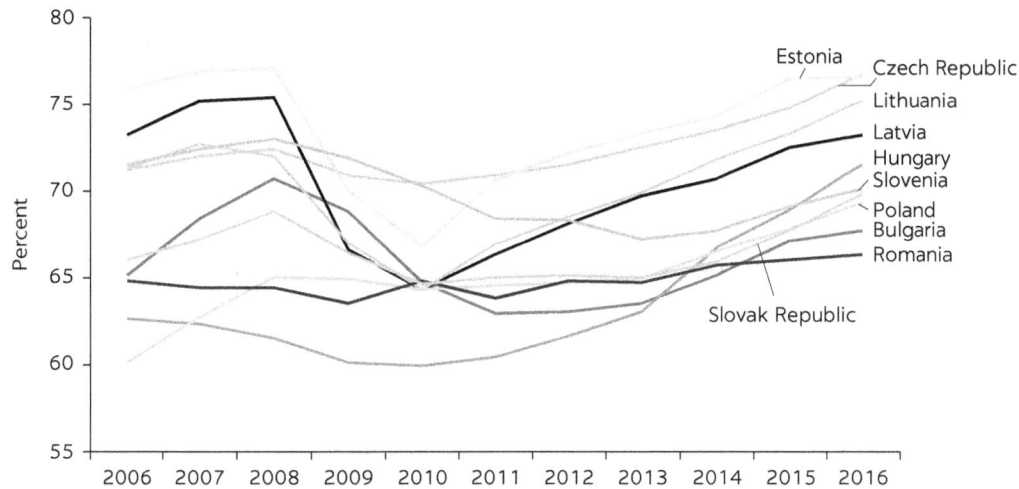

Source: Eurostat.
Note: Figure shows the employment rate for ages 20–64.

not only for market integration, but also for job creation and shared prosperity.

Several factors may explain the low variability of the employment and unemployment rates (latter not shown): after the early stages of transition, when job shedding from existing enterprises outweighed job creation (World Bank 2014a), employment had just started to grow when the crisis hit, and recovery has been slow since then. Agriculture continues to be the employer of last resort, as labor market adjustment of low-skilled workers occurs mainly at the margin of the sector, and not by status changes to unemployment or inactivity. This is also consistent with the high labor force participation rate in lagging regions.

The recent improvement in the overall employment rate coincides with the postcrisis recovery in the manufacturing, construction, and trade sectors, which is to a large extent fueled by a boost in private consumption and thus is unlikely to be sustainable in the long run. Labor market gains of low-skilled workers are achieved primarily through movements to nontradable sectors such as construction and trade, which are demand-constrained and sensitive to cycles. Continued human capital challenges are holding back systematic transitions to higher-productivity jobs, and many people remain a shock away from slipping back into poverty, as observed most recently during the financial crisis. Expanding the set of economic opportunities is vital to achieving a robust middle-class society.

A broader labor shortage points toward the need to address structural factors that impede the mobilization of available labor and access to jobs, in particular for women, youth, and minorities. The activity gap for women is especially large and has been on the rise. Striking a balance between potentially conflicting objectives of labor market and family policies can be difficult; however, it appears that existing policies reinforce the low activity rate of women (box 3.1). Romanian women are the youngest to marry in the EU, which, combined with a generous maternity leave and a severe lack of formal child care, has the unintended effect of keeping prime-age women out of the labor market for a prolonged period. The lack of part-time jobs makes returning to the labor market

BOX 3.1

A reverse gender gap?

A closer look at gender disparities reveals an interesting dichotomy along the urban–rural divide. A large gender gap exists in labor force participation, driven by rural women with less than tertiary education. These women have lower skills, marry about 3 years earlier than urban women—in a country in the EU where women are the youngest to marry—and have a much lower probability of working throughout their lives. Strong gender norms persist, consistent with the story of a country that has a large population left behind in rural areas. The issue is magnified for Roma women.

At the tertiary level, there are no differences in participation regardless of location and age group. On the contrary, there is evidence of a reverse gender gap, as girls outperform boys in all subjects of the Programme for International Student Assessment (PISA) test, and tertiary enrollment today is higher among women. Interestingly, women are overrepresented in traditionally male-dominated occupations in the fields of science, math, and ICT—much more so than in other EU countries—alongside the usual fields of health and education.

An explanation could be that this is a coping strategy of women in an environment that is still dominated by strong norms, but where women have increasingly better skills. Those highly skilled, mostly urban, women gravitate toward these "hard" fields as the work is more technical, with less scope for social intervention that could exacerbate gender gaps, and that likely offer better work-life balance.

even harder, especially for low-skilled, entry-level jobs that are likely to be bound by the high cost of creating a formal job and minimum wages set for full-time equivalent jobs. There is also an acute need for long-term care in a rapidly aging society where 35 percent of the population lives with a senior age 65 and older. Strong gender norms dictate that the care burden falls disproportionately on women.

Only about a quarter of youth are employed, and one in five is neither in employment nor in education and training (NEET), the latter driven by the high early school leaving rate. Two thirds of NEETs are inactive, and include a high share of Roma and women in rural areas. Activation policies that are tailored to the specific barriers to work could benefit these groups greatly. In addition to the Youth Guarantee,[11] which has reached only a partial group of NEETs, comprehensive measures and budgets were adopted recently that could support activation.[12]

Further, introducing job-search responsibilities and access to active labor market policies to beneficiaries of the Minimum Social Insertion Income (MSII) program could provide strong incentives for poor people to return to work. The institutional capacity and resources of the National Agency for Employment need to be improved, with a focus on providing local employment services in rural marginalized communities where the share of nonworking adults is high.

Underutilization and misallocation of labor is high, as a large share of labor is trapped in low-productivity agricultural and other informal activities. Many of the working poor face low earnings because of their dependence on income from sources other than the formal, private, or public sectors— notably subsistence farming and other informal activities.

Agriculture, construction, and trade appear to have very high rates of informal employment, which, owing to the sectoral employment distribution, impacts the bottom 40 disproportionately (table 3.2).[13] Informal employment, especially

TABLE 3.2 **Informal employment rates are very high in agriculture, construction, and trade**

Thousands

SECTOR	EMPLOYMENT		% INFORMAL
	LFS	SBR	
Agriculture	2,184	137	93.7%
Construction	636	324	49.1%
Trade	1,149	817	28.9%
Financial activities	105	102	2.2%
Other	4,461	3,800	14.8%
TOTAL	8,535	5,180	39.3%

Source: National Institute of Statistics.
Note: Employment figures are from Labor Force Survey (LFS) and Statistical Business Registry (SBR) (in 1,000s). Data for 2015.

if involuntary, is associated with low productivity, low earnings, inferior working conditions including fewer benefits, and lower well-being.[14] This area requires further attention, as available data and evidence limits the understanding of the institutional drivers and welfare consequences of informality in Romania, and therefore the range of policy responses. The roles of rising minimum wages and employment protection legislation need to be carefully examined.

Reducing poverty requires tackling the large productivity gap in the agricultural sector. Agriculture still accounts for about 25 percent of employment, yet contributes only 4 percent to GDP. Agricultural producers have a poverty rate of 51 percent as of 2015.[15] Romania has not been able to establish a viable, commercially-oriented farming sector, despite its arable land representing 38 percent of the surface area. Romania's large utilized agricultural area stands out in the EU for its low productivity, because of highly fragmented farm structures, high levels of informality, weak financial intermediation, and low access to credit. In this regard, completing the cadaster—another area where resolving institutional challenges is critical—would allow for significant progress in these areas. The recent rapid growth in the agri-finance market signals the need for continuous agricultural investments and for working with nontraditional investors (for example, nonbank financial institutions and microfinancial institutions) to reach MSMEs and small farmers in particular. Other constraints to increasing agricultural productivity include the reliance on outdated labor-intensive technologies, the low quality of human capital, deficient extension services, and low expenditure on research and development (World Bank 2018a).

The role of sustainable agribusiness is key to upgrading farming activity through a renewed focus on developing and strengthening competitive value chains, enhancing access to markets and regional integration, and thus improving productivity and rural livelihoods. Ailing infrastructure is adding to the cost of doing business in the sector, and is a crucial constraint to improving regional integration through sustainable agribusiness. As an example, the port of Constanta's role in materializing the export potential of the agricultural sector is essential: about 80 percent of the country's grain production is exported through the port, but its small capacity causes a significant backlog. Private sector potential could be leveraged to improve infrastructure, export competitiveness, and rural livelihoods. Concurrently, it is necessary to retrain displaced workers through vocational and lifelong learning programs (World Bank 2018a).

FIGURE 3.10

There is a spatial mismatch between people and jobs

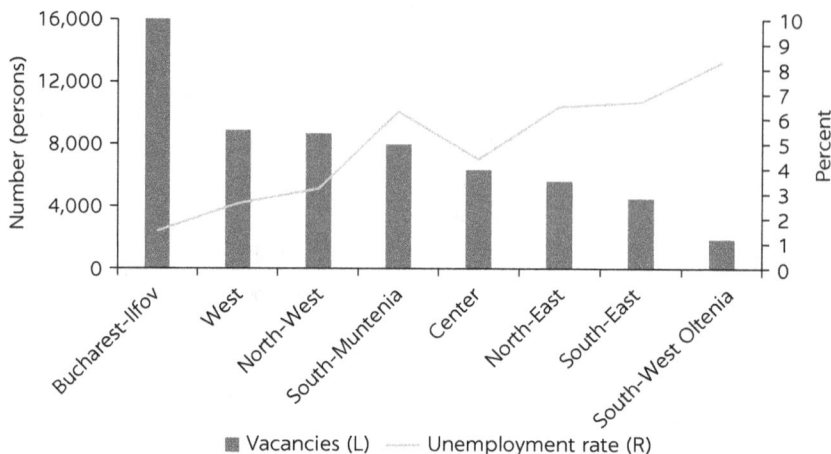

◼ Vacancies (L) —— Unemployment rate (R)

Source: National Institute of Statistics.

Spatial and skills mismatches constrain job growth and productivity enhancing labor reallocation. As signs of spatial mismatch, unemployment is higher in lagging regions where there are fewer available jobs (figure 3.10). Yet Romania has the lowest residential mobility in the EU, with less than 2 percent of the population moving internally over a five-year period.[16] This is in stark contrast to the EU average of 18 percent. Greater internal mobility toward urban centers of economic activity would foster local agglomeration economies and increase returns to assets. With virtually almost everyone living in owner-occupied homes (98 percent), real estate markets remain underdeveloped and limit the conversion of immovable assets into usable wealth, further constraining mobility. An important institutional constraint to this is the prevalence of informal property rights. Accessibility to jobs and opportunities is a function of proximity and mobility, but the infrastructure gap is large, especially in rural areas. ICT connectivity and digital skills are lagging even more, with less than a third of rural households connected to the internet.

Many employers identify the need for stronger socio-emotional, job-related skills over technical skills that can be transitory. The lack of relevant skills is related to the challenges of an education system that is struggling with high underachievement, large urban-rural disparities, and outdated curricula, and frequently leads to weak labor market attachment. VET qualifications and curricula are not sufficiently attuned to labor market needs (EC 2016). Notably, estimates of returns to education across EU countries suggest that Romania is the only country where the wage premium to tertiary education appears to have fallen significantly in the last decade.[17] This is unusual given the shortage of highly skilled labor and is suggestive of a demand-side issue that may warrant further investigation.

Increases in minimum wages have only a limited impact on the earnings of the bottom 40, but the potential cost could be high if it is not accompanied by corresponding increases in labor productivity. Minimum wages have been increasing steeply, most recently by 31 percent to 1900 RON, which puts them at about half of average gross wages. Relatively few in the bottom 40 hold formal jobs that would benefit from minimum wage increases. The latter is partly propelling the rise in real wages, which surpassed the pace of labor productivity, causing concerns that this could hamper job creation, erode competitiveness, and foster incentives for informal jobs.[18] A recent study showed that Romania's minimum-wage setting framework is among the least predictable in the EU, indicating that a transparent mechanism based on objective criteria is needed (Arpaia et al. 2017). Given the low benefits but potentially high costs, the policy should be exercised with great caution.

EQUITY REQUIRES A ROBUST SOCIAL SAFETY NET FOR THOSE FALLING BEHIND, AND HIGH-QUALITY PUBLIC SERVICES FOR ALL

Social safety nets are vital in their role to provide protection from various risks; yet social spending is low, inefficient, and increasingly skewed toward pensions, making it less effective at reaching the ones most in need. Romania's spending on social protection benefits was at 14.4 percent of GDP, making it the second-lowest in the EU. With an aging population, social protection spending is bound to become skewed toward old-age benefits: in fact, Romania's dependency rate is projected to double over the next four decades (World Bank 2015).

Social transfers are characterized by a prevalence of categorical programs, rendering them ineffective at reducing poverty. The MSII Program is expected to consolidate existing means-tested programs, including Guaranteed Minimum Income, the Family Benefit, and the Heating Benefit, improve targeting, increase coverage and benefit levels, and introduce work incentives into the benefits formula. However, implementation continues to be delayed.

Social services that involve social protection, employment, education, and healthcare are fragmented and sparse in rural areas. Integrated social services are lacking for the poorest and most marginalized groups, as social services are not effectively linked with cash benefits for poor households who also face various barriers to accessing the benefits. Needs assessments and management information systems are not used to inform local policies and practice. Meanwhile, social housing is disconnected from other social assistance, severely underfinanced, and unable to meet local demands. The quality of the housing stock is very low, exposing inhabitants to potential health risks. A harmonized policy to support people with disabilities is lacking, the deinstitutionalization of adults in residential care has been slow, and the transition to community-based services remains a priority (World Bank 2015). Romania still has one of the largest number of children in the child protection system in the region, though progress is being made in transferring children from institutional to community-based care (World Bank 2014c).

The pension system needs to move toward a system that is sustainable, fair, and equitable to all contributors, and sufficient to prevent old-age poverty, while providing benefits that are reasonable in relation to contributions made. Ad hoc adjustments in pension benefits helped a large number of people escape poverty before the crisis, but this driver is now largely exhausted.[19]

Contributory pensions, when considered transfers, are the most powerful redistributive instrument, but there are growing concerns for equity. Pensions account for a little more than half of the redistributive impact of fiscal policies (direct taxes, transfers, and pensions) on the reduction of income inequality (World Bank 2017b). However, pension coverage is low among the bottom 40, who are largely excluded from formal jobs, and has been falling steadily in rural areas, mainly due to falling coverage under the old farmers pension scheme. The latter exacerbates the inequities of a system that is heavily subsidized by state funds. Further, frequent changes to the system and the benefit formula result in different benefit levels for similarly positioned individuals. Another source of inequity is the very high levels of pensions for the military, police, Parliament, judges, and prosecutors, for whom benefit levels can exceed 100 percent of preretirement pay. Such inequities need to be resolved urgently.

The cadaster system is an important area of unfinished reforms, with wide-ranging development consequences. Informal property rights are still the norm, with only 15 percent of rural and 51 percent of urban real estate registered as of 2015 (World Bank 2015). The consequences of low property registration are deep, and include the underdevelopment of real estate markets, inequitable property taxation, and thus low revenues, low investment and access to credit that limit firm growth, inefficient spatial planning and development, poor public infrastructure, and underutilization of state assets and EU funds. An evocative example of dysfunctional land markets is given by the Esplanada site, which is a prime real estate location in Bucharest. Despite many attempts, its development continues to be hampered by unresolved ownership issues.[20]

Albeit slow and with substantial regional heterogeneity, progress is being made in real estate registration, and further improvements are expected under the National Program for Cadaster and Land Book, with strong commitment from the implementing agency. Importantly, given the political environment, notarial involvement in registration should be reserved for cases where the need can be demonstrated, and systematic registration can be based on the available evidence and powers of the process to adjudicate rights with broad community participation and oversight (World Bank 2014d).

Finally, the provision of high-quality public services remains an urgent priority, especially in rural areas. About 4.5 million people (22 percent) lack access to piped potable water and 6 million (32 percent) live without flush toilets, which could lead to significant public health risks and compares unfavorably even to neighboring non-EU countries. Most of the gap is in rural areas (World Bank 2017a). Ninety percent of rural dwellings rely on biomass for household heating, which is costly, inefficient, and polluting. Moreover, energy poverty is at a substantial 25–40 percent with up to 100,000 households lacking access to electricity. District heating is often the only viable option for poor and vulnerable consumers, especially in urban areas. For this reason, optimization of the district heating system is particularly urgent, as the financial sustainability of the system is being undermined by consumers opting out (World Bank 2018c).

NOTES

1. In this chapter, poverty refers to the anchored AROP (at-risk-of-poverty) rate, for which the poverty line is defined at 60 percent of median income from the income distribution reported in EU-SILC 2008 and deflated across survey years.
2. The shared prosperity premium is calculated as the difference between the mean income growth of the bottom and the total population.
3. Most of the gap is in rural areas where the coverage is at 76 percent.
4. The minimum benefits package covers life-threatening emergencies, epidemic-prone and infectious diseases, and care during pregnancy.
5. Source: EUROSTAT. Accessed March 31, 2018.

6. These include the Romanian National Health Strategy 2014–2010, the Strategy to Reduce Early School Leaving 2015–2020, National Strategy for Tertiary Education 2015–2020 and the National Strategy for Lifelong Learning 2015–2020. A Strategy for modernizing education infrastructure was also finalized recently.
7. "Children left behind" refers to children with one or more parent that migrated abroad for work. The National Authority for the Protection of Rights of the Child (ANPDCA) collects statistics on these children based on self-reports, which is likely to be underestimated.
8. UNICEF (2008) estimated the number of children left behind at 350,000.
9. Under the European Roma Integration Framework, Romania has prepared its National Roma Integration Strategy 2015–2020 (NRIS) that aims to gradually eliminate the poverty and social exclusion of Roma by stepping up its programs and policies in the areas of education, employment, healthcare, and housing. The NRIS can be considered an important step toward achieving the national targets assumed under the Europe 2020 Strategy.
10. Investment in cities—as sources of productivity growth, human capital accumulation, and ultimately as locations of opportunity—is central to achieving the objectives of policies for lagging regions. Beyond the competitiveness of the city, the degree to which improved conditions spill over to lagging regions—through migration, commuting, regional supply chains, and service delivery linkages—matters (World Bank 2018f).
11. The Youth Guarantee is a commitment by EU member states to ensure that all young people under the age of 25 years receive a good-quality offer of employed, continued education, apprenticeship, or traineeship within four months of becoming unemployed or leaving formal education.
12. The Ministry of Labor has for the first time an integrated overview of the European Social Fund and national budgets for active labor market policies. Take-up is expected to improve, thanks to a mix of more attractive demand and supply-side activation measures (including support for entrepreneurship and employment subsidies), tailor-made for groups furthest from the labor market. Financial incentives covering relocation and transport costs were increased to improve internal labor mobility in line with the national mobility plan (European Commission 2017).
13. This measure of informal employment is constructed using official employment statistics from Labor Force Surveys and employment figures from the Statistical Business Register. The latter captures employment in legally registered entities. Similar measures have been used in Russia (see Gimpelson and Kaliushnikov 2014).
14. The literature has approached informality from two opposing viewpoints. The "exclusion" view posits that workers and firms prefer to be in the formal sector, but are involuntarily excluded because of limited opportunities. The "exit" view presumes that informality is partly a choice of individuals and firms because the costs of formalization outweigh the benefits (Perry et al. 2007). Informality is a complex phenomenon and can be defined in different ways: the European Commission committed to reducing "undeclared work" which is defined as "paid activities that are lawful in nature but not declared to public authorities" (EC 2014).
15. Staff calculation using EU–SILC 2016.
16. EUROSTAT. People in the EU—statistics on geographic mobility.
17. Estimates are based on EUSILC data.
18. In general, the impact of minimum wage increases on employment has been found modest in the past; there have been significant negative employment effects when the minimum wage was quite high or out of line with economic conditions. (Betcherman 2014). There is little empirical evidence on the impact of minimum wages; however, during SCD consultations, the potential adverse impact on jobs and businesses was raised frequently. Specific examples included factories being relocated across the border to Serbia, where wages are lower.
19. Romania underwent several significant pension reforms since 2000. Following a reform in 2004 that introduced several measures to improve fiscal sustainability, in 2007 Parliament approved measures to address declining benefit levels (and essentially reversed some of the previous reforms). These measures, implemented in two phases, included increases in pension point values in November 2007 and again in October 2008 (European Commission 2012). As a result, per capita government expenditure on old-age pension beneficiaries increased 88 percent between 2006 and 2011 (ESPROSS, accessed April 16, 2017).
20. See World Bank (2017c) for details.

REFERENCES

Arpaia A., Pedro Cardoso, Aron Kiss, Kristine Van Herck, and Anneleen Vandeplas. 2017. "Statutory Minimum Wages in the EU: Institutional Settings and Macroeconomic Implications." Policy Paper No. 124, February 2017, Institute for the Study of Labor (IZA), Bonn, Germany.

Betcherman, Gordon. 2014. "Labor Market Regulations: What Do We Know about Their Impacts in Developing Countries?" *The World Bank Research Observer* 30: 124–53.

Bussolo, Maurizio and Luis-Felipe Lopez-Calva, 2014. *Shared Prosperity: Paving the Way in Europe and Central Asia.* Washington, DC: World Bank.

Checchi, Daniele, Vito Peragine, and Laura Serlenga. 2016. "Inequality of Opportunity in Europe: Is There a Role for Institutions?" In *Inequality: Causes and Consequences*, edited by Lorenzo Cappellari, Solomon W. Polachek, and Konstantinos Tatsiramos, in *Research in Labor Economics*, Volume 43: 1–44.

Corak, Miles. 2013. "Income Inequality, Equality of Opportunity, and Intergenerational Mobility." *Journal of Economic Perspectives* 27 (3), Summer 2013: 79–102.

EC (European Commission). 2012. *Pension Adequacy in the EU 2010–2050*, by the Directorate-General for Employment, Social Affairs and Inclusion of the European Commission and the Social Protection Committee. Luxembourg: OECD.

EC (European Commission). 2014. *Special Eurobarometer 402: Undeclared Work in the European Union.* Luxembourg: OECD.

——. 2016. *Education and Training Monitor: Romania.* Luxembourg: OECD.

——. 2017. *Youth Guarantee Country by Country: Romania.* Luxemborug: OECD.

FRA (European Union Agency for Fundamental Rights). 2016. *Second European Union Minorities and Discrimination Survey. Roma - selected findings.* Luxembourg: OECD.

Gimpelson, Vladimir and Rostislav Kapeliushnikov. 2014. "Between Light and Shadow: Informality in the Russian Labour Market." Discussion Paper No. 8279, June 2014. Institute for the Study of Labor (IZA), Bonn, Germany.

Grigoli, Francesco and Adrian Robles. 2017. "Inequality Overhang." Working Paper No. 76, March, International Monetary Fund., Washington, DC.

Hardy, Wojciech, Roma Keister and Piotr Lewandowski. 2016. "Technology or Upskilling? Trends in the Task Composition of Jobs in Central and Eastern Europe." Working Paper No. 1, Institute for Structural Research (IBS), Warsaw, Poland.

OECD. 2016. PISA 2015 Results (Volume I): Excellence and Equity in Education, PISA, Paris: OECD Publishing.

——. 2017. *The Governance of Inclusive Growth.* Paris: OECD Publishing.

Perry, Guillermo, et al. 2007. *Informality: Exit and Exclusion.* World Bank Latin American and Caribbean Studies. Washington, DC: World Bank.

UNICEF. 2008. *National Analysis of Children Left Behind by Parents Who Migrated Abroad for Employment*, by Alexandru Toth et al. Research report. New York: UNICEF.

World Bank. 2010. *Roma Inclusion: An Economic Opportunity for Bulgaria, Czech Republic, Romania and Serbia.* Washington, DC: World Bank.

——. 2014a. *Back to work: growing with jobs in Europe and Central Asia.* Europe and Central Asia Reports. Washington, DC: World Bank Group.

——. 2014b. *Diagnostics and policy advice for supporting Roma inclusion in Romania.* Washington, DC: World Bank Group.

——. 2014c. Romania: Children in Public Care. Washington, DC: World Bank Group.

——. 2014d. *Draft National Strategy for Systematic and Sporadic Real Estate Registration.* Washington, DC: World Bank Group.

——. 2015. *Background Study for the National Strategy on Social Inclusion and Poverty Reduction 2015-2020.* Washington, DC: World Bank Group.

——. 2016. *Pinpointing poverty in Romania.* Washington, DC: World Bank Group.

——. 2017a. *Romania Water Diagnostic*. Washington, DC: World Bank Group.

——. 2017b. "Fiscal redistribution in the European Union." In *Growing United: Upgrading Europe's Convergence machine*. Washington, DC: World Bank Group.

——. 2017c. *Magnet Cities: Migration and Commuting in Romania*. Washington, DC: World Bank Group.

——. 2018a. Background Note for the Romania Systematic Country Diagnostic. Agriculture.

——. 2018b. Background Note for the Romania Systematic Country Diagnostic. Education.

——. 2018c. Background Note for the Romania Systematic Country Diagnostic. Energy Sector.

——. 2018d. Background Note for the Romania Systematic Country Diagnostic. Health Sector.

——. 2018e. Background Note for the Romania Systematic Country Diagnostic. Roma Inclusion.

——. 2018f. *Rethinking Lagging Regions: Using Cohesion Policy to Deliver on the Potential of Europe's Regions*. Washington, DC: World Bank Group.

World Economic Forum. 2016. *The Future of Jobs. Employment, Skills and Workforce Strategy for the Fourth Industrial Revolution*. Global Challenge Insight Report.

World Health Organization. 2016. *Romania Health System Review*. Health Systems in Transition series. Geneva: WHO.

4 Improving Resilience to Natural Hazards and Climate Change

NATURAL HAZARDS, SUCH AS CLIMATE RISKS AND EARTHQUAKES, POSE A GREAT CHALLENGE TO THE ROMANIAN ECONOMY

Romania stands out for its vulnerability to risks from earthquakes, floods, and droughts—the latter two intensified by climate change. Since 1990, 77 severe disaster events[1] were recorded across the country, resulting in more than US$3.5 billion (in current US$) of direct damage, or 3.5 percent of average GDP over the period.[2] Estimates of the overall impact of climate-related hazards in Romania indicate that expected annual damage to infrastructure alone would double by 2020, and by 2080 could be six times higher.[3]

Natural disasters and climate risks disproportionately affect poorer counties. Even though provinces such as Bucuresti, Prahova and Buzau are at greatest risk of earthquakes in terms of absolute GDP losses, the most affected in terms of normalized annual average of affected GDP[4] are Braila and Vrancea, which are also the provinces with significantly lower GDP. And the counties most economically impacted by floods (in terms of normalized annual average of affected GDP) are Ialomita, Satu Mare and Teleorman—also the counties with a lower GDP relative to the rest of the country (map 4.1).

The potential damage to natural, physical, and human assets can curtail economic growth, jeopardize fiscal sustainability, and negatively affect the well-being of Romania's population. Given the extent of damage resulting from these disasters, and the current policy, legal, institutional, and investment environment that is exacerbating related losses, improving social and economic resilience is critical to achieving sustainable and inclusive growth in Romania.[5]

This chapter draws extensively on World Bank (2018) and on World Bank (2017a).

MAP 4.1

Losses from floods and earthquakes are greatest in the counties with significantly lower GDP

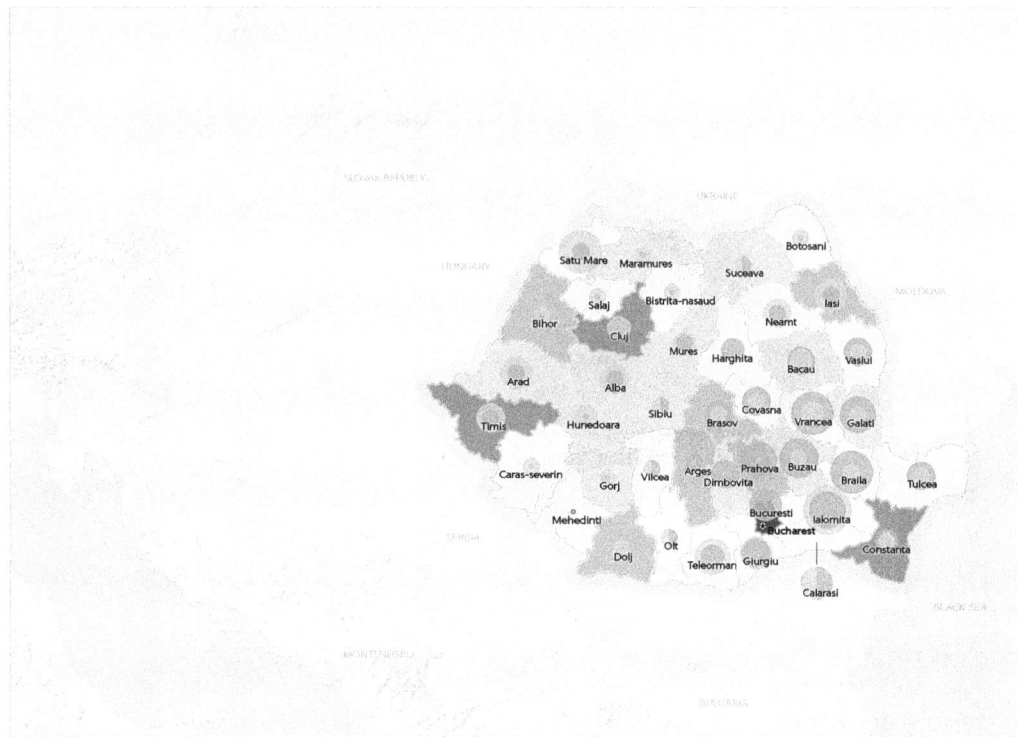

Source: Romania Country Risk Profile, GFDRR, World Bank.

BOX 4.1

Romania is more vulnerable to natural risks than other EU countries

Romania faces double the risk to assets and socio-economic activity from disasters compared with Poland, for example. Seventy percent of assets of the poor are vulnerable to destruction, compared with 43 percent in Poland, and even the assets of nonpoor people in Romania have three times the vulnerability compared with Poland. Meanwhile, 80 percent of the population have access to early warning in Romania, compared with 100 percent in Poland.

Risk assessments usually focus on: hazard—the probability that an event occurs; exposure—the population and assets located in the affected area; and asset vulnerability—the fraction of asset value lost when affected by a hazard. These factors constitute the risk to assets, in monetary terms, which is the average value of the damages that natural disasters such as floods or earthquakes inflict on assets—often measured in their replacement or repair value (Hallegatte et al. 2017).

EARTHQUAKES COULD DERAIL ECONOMIC GROWTH

Bucharest has the highest seismic risk of all capital cities in Europe, and is one of the 10 most vulnerable cities in the world (Armaş et al., 2017). This is because of Bucharest's proximity to the Vrancea earthquake zone. In the last five centuries, there have been, on average, two magnitude 7+ earthquakes each century, with five earthquakes since 1802 with magnitudes higher than 7.5 (Armaş et al., 2017).[6] Moreover, at a global level, in a ranking of countries with the highest amount of built-up surface potentially exposed to seismic hazards, two European countries emerge: Italy and Romania, with 84 percent and 92 percent of built-up surfaces in hazard zones respectively (European Commission, 2017). An overview of historical seismicity in Romania is presented in map 4.2.

Thousands of lives have been lost, and tens of thousands of buildings have been damaged by earthquakes in Romania over the last 200 years.[7] Over the last 100 years alone, 13 earthquakes resulted in 2,630 fatalities and affected more than 400,000 people. The 1977 earthquake, measuring 7.2 on the Richter scale, caused more than 1,500 fatalities, left 11,321 injured, and collapsed or severely damaged 156,000 residential apartments, in addition to damages to public facilities such as schools and hospitals. The World Bank (1978) reported an estimated total damage of US$2 billion,[8] with Bucharest accounting for 70 percent of the total damage—approximately US$1.4 billion (World Bank, 1978). The 1977 earthquake contributed extensively to the serious economic crisis that began in Romania in 1979 (Pavel, 2016).

With Bucharest and surrounding areas being exposed to high earthquake risks, the potential damage of a future earthquake could have significant consequences for the national economy. More than 75 percent of the population (and 65 percent of the urban population) are vulnerable to earthquakes, and 45 percent of all national response support is in areas with high earthquake hazards. Furthermore, 60–75 percent of fixed assets and 70–80 percent of GDP is estimated to be produced in earthquake- prone areas (General Inspectorate for Emergency Situations, 2016). Lastly, urbanization and the increased concentration of economic assets in earthquake-prone areas suggest that the risk will continue to grow over time, and will likely double by 2080 (World Bank, 2017c).

MAP 4.2

Historical seismic activity has occurred near densely populated areas

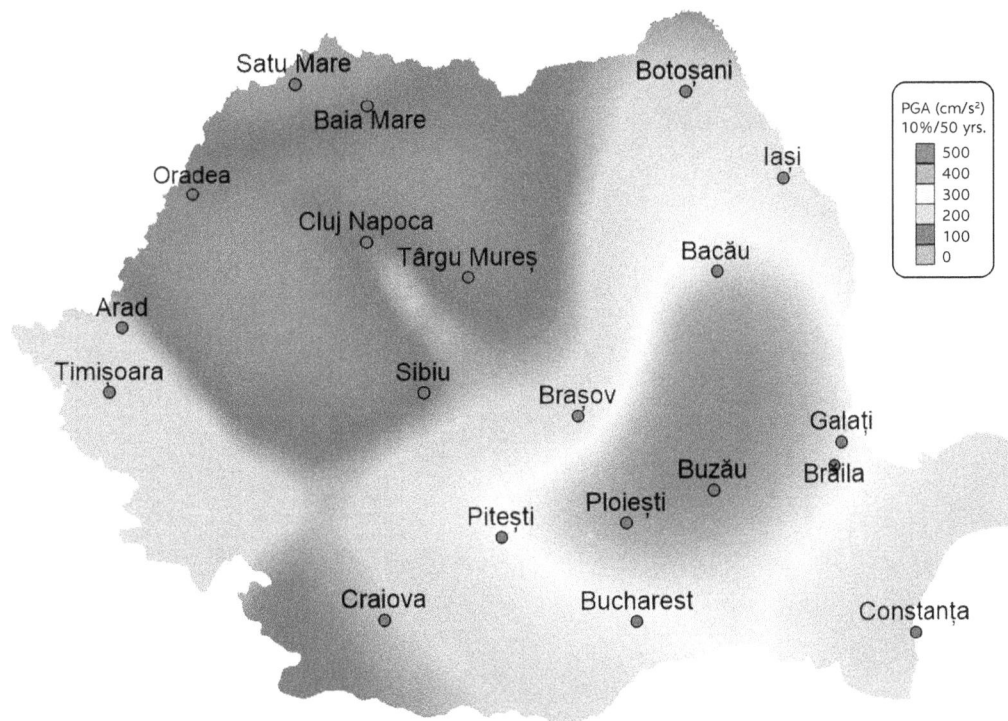

Source: World Bank.

Romania has made progress in improving preparedness and ability to mitigate seismic risks. Romania is in the process of strengthening legislative and organizational frameworks for disaster mitigation and preparedness, and is also making efforts to develop national and regional risk management plans to incorporate risk reduction approaches. However, given the potential magnitude of impacts in the event of a future earthquake, there is a need to strengthen protection for households, including through deepening the insurance coverage against the cost of damage associated with earthquakes, and to prioritize investments in seismic risk reduction, including through seismic retrofitting of structurally unsafe residential buildings. There is also an urgent need to ensure that buildings and infrastructure that provide critical public services—such as emergency facilities, schools, public administration buildings, electricity, communications, and water services—are resilient to earthquakes.

FLOOD RISK IS INCREASING

Romania has seen an increasing frequency of floods in the last decades. Romania's flood risk is higher than all other countries in the Balkan region, while among the EU countries, only Poland, the Czech Republic, and Slovak Republic are at greater risks of floods. Floods have occurred in 9 of the past 15 years—2005 being an exceptional year, with floods occurring in almost all river basins. The increase in frequency could be associated with both the anthropogenic activities that changed or reduced the space of rivers, and climate change impacts (World Bank, 2017a).

The frequency of flash floods has also been increasing. In the past 25 years, flash floods have expanded in their spatial coverage, particularly in the Eastern (Transylvania) and Southwest regions (Dobrogea) (map 4.3). The increased frequency of flash floods is linked to an evolving pattern of changes in the intensity

MAP 4.3

The frequency of flash floods has been increasing, particularly in Eastern and Southwest regions of Romania

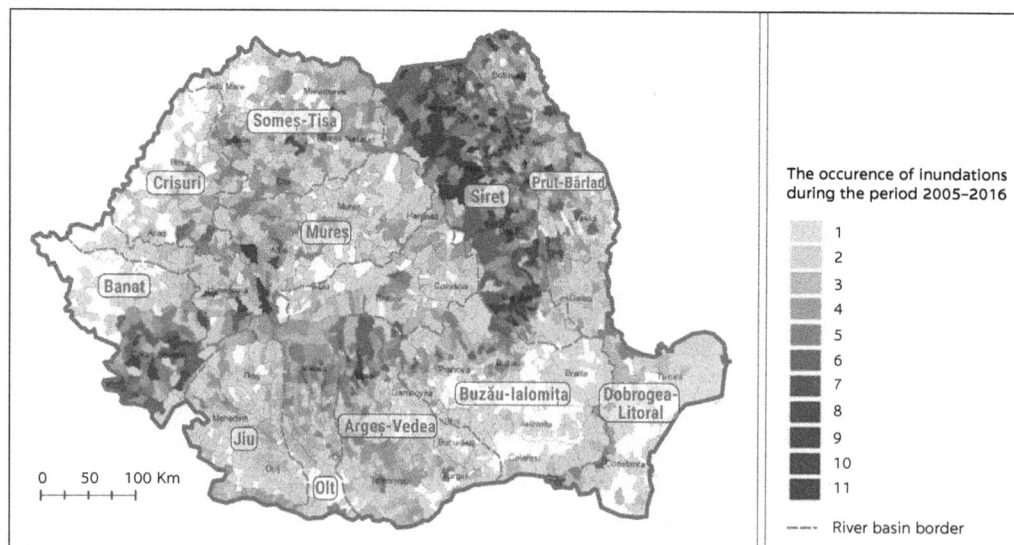

Source: World Bank, based on Romanian Waters National Administration, ANAR 2017.

and distribution of heavy rainstorms associated with climate change and defor-estation (World Bank, 2017a). Larger areas of formerly afforested land have been aggressively harvested through abusive, and in many cases illegal, logging. This has left the slopes exposed to heavy rains, and without the previous soil and veg-etation retention capacity for water.

Total damages caused by floods during 2002–2013 are estimated at EUR 6.3 billion, the 7th largest in the EU. In the same period, as a result of floods, Romania suffered from the largest death toll —183 fatalities—and the highest total number of destroyed houses—43,900—across Europe (World Bank, 2017a). The 2010 historic floods alone affected 12,237 people, caused 26 deaths, and at least EUR 1.1 billion in damage (General Inspectorate for Emergency Situations, 2016), amounting to 0.6 percent of GDP. The southeast, northwest, and western parts of the country have been the most affected, with considerable impact on local GDP—more than 4 percent of local GDP on average.[9] Moreover, in the counties of Satu Mare in the Northwest and Ialomita in the Southeast, the average reduction of local GDP from flood events exceeds 8 percent.

Climate change is expected to further exacerbate Romania's already high risk of floods. As precipitation patterns become more irregular, and the frequency of shorter, more intense, localized rainfall events becomes more common, flood events are also projected to occur more frequently in many river basins, particu-larly in winter and spring (Romania, Ministry of Environment and Climate Change, 2013).

Romania has made considerable investments in the flood management frame-work and infrastructure. As a result, in terms of the proportion of GDP affected by floods, Romania does better than many other EU countries less prone to floods, such as Slovenia, Latvia, Lithuania, Croatia, or Hungary. The lower dam-ages from floods after 2010 can be attributed to both climatic conditions and the initial outcomes of the implementation of the actions encompassed by the EU Flood Management Directive—especially for improved warning systems. As part of the implementation of EU Floods Directive, the Romanian Waters National Administration (ANAR) has developed a methodology for determining potential flood risk areas that allows for spatial mapping of flood risks based on hydrolog-ical data collected. However, the methodology does not account for climate change impacts or anthropic interventions in the basin (World Bank, 2017a).

RECURRING DROUGHTS DISPROPORTIONATELY AFFECT RURAL LIVELIHOODS

Romania is highly vulnerable to increasing occurrences of droughts, which lead to lower agricultural production and income. Droughts have affected 48 percent of agricultural land already, with estimates suggesting a 20 percent chance of severe drought in the next 10 years.[10] The South (The Romanian Plain, Getic Plateau), Southeast (Dobrogea) and East (Moldavian Plateau) are highly vulnerable to droughts.

The occurrence of droughts in the past has adversely impacted Romania's economy through drought-induced declines in agricultural production and in the incomes of the most vulnerable individuals. The drought of 2007 was the most severe drought of the last 60 years and significantly affected agricultural activity because of insufficient water reserves and poorly functioning irrigation systems. Moreover, a total of eight drought months were recorded during the agricultural year of 2011–2012, while November 2011 was the driest month in the last 52 years in Romania, with a monthly mean of only 1.2 mm of rainfall, versus a multi-annual mean of 43.9 mm. Agricultural production and rural areas are particularly affected by the incidence of droughts, and studies suggest a 40–60 percent decline in crop yields during times of drought.[11] In fact, there was a significant decline in agricultural income in 2007 and 2012, the years of severe droughts in Romania (figure 4.1). In 2012 alone, the downfall of gross value-added in the agricultural sector was of 21.2 percent, with drought being one of the major factors that led to a decrease in GDP (World Bank, 2017a).

Projected increases in temperature and changes in precipitation patterns are expected to lead to more frequent and persistent heat waves, coupled with stronger and more spatially-extended droughts. Increases in annual average temperatures are expected to be between 0.5°C and 1.5°C by 2029, and between 2.0°C and 5.0°C by 2099, depending on the global climate scenario used (Romania, Ministry of Environment and Climate Change, 2013). The increase in the frequency and magnitude of droughts in several parts of the country is most notable in the Southeast, which concentrates most of the arable land, and where a semi-arid climate will gradually be established over the next 2 to 3 decades. Moreover, a study conducted by the EU Joint Research Center in 2014 demonstrated that Central and Southern Europe (including France, Austria, Czech Republic, Slovak Republic, Hungary, Slovenia, and Romania) will be the second-most-affected regions in the European Union. This is because of the decrease in precipitation by approximately 24.4 percent during summer season, which increases exposure to drought and leads to losses rising to 3 percent of annual regional GDP (World Bank, 2017a).

Agricultural production and the livelihoods of Romania's population in rural areas will be particularly affected by droughts. Livestock and crop production typically bear approximately 80 percent of the damage and loss caused by droughts, and the agricultural sector bears 25 percent of the damages and losses caused by all climate-related disasters. (FAO, 2015). Moreover, since irrigation

FIGURE 4.1

Agricultural factor income was affected by droughts in 2007 and 2012

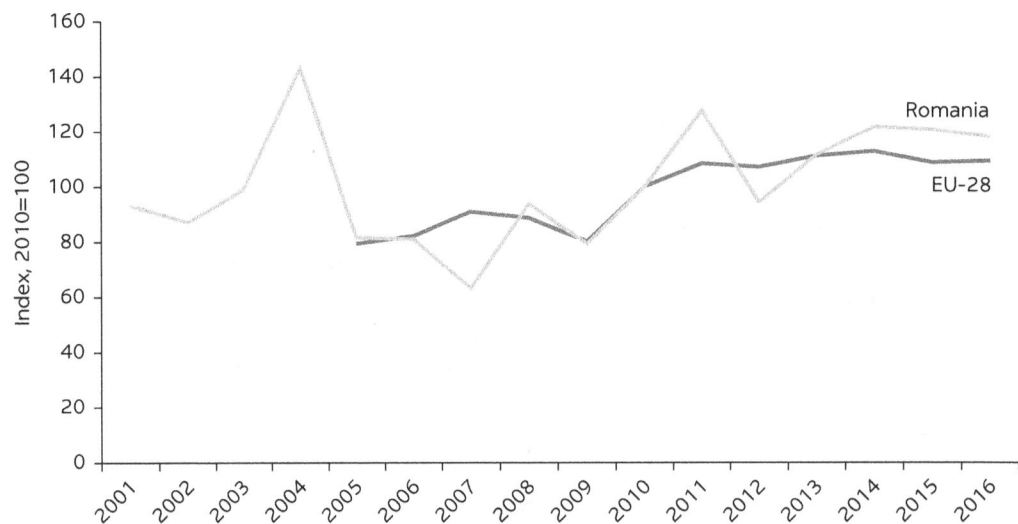

Source: EC services, Eurostat.
Note: Agricultural income per annual work unit (AWU), 2001–16, index (2010=100). It corresponds to the deflated (real) net value added at factor cost of agriculture.

infrastructure is lacking[12] and largely unaffordable by the poor, it will be critical to offset rain deficits in the country's semi-arid southern and eastern regions and to address the climate risks affecting agriculture.

Romania made significant efforts to address vulnerability in the agricultural sector, recognizing that there is no trade-off between resilience and agricultural productivity growth in the country. The modernization of agriculture will increase productivity and make the sector more resilient to climate change. Under projected climate change scenarios, improving crop varieties and moving from rain-fed to irrigated farming are not only economically viable, but also yield-increasing choices. Along with averting declines in production, mitigating the impacts of climate-risk-related disasters would prevent declines in farmers' incomes, bolstering rural livelihoods and food security.

THE POLICY, LEGAL, INSTITUTIONAL, AND INVESTMENT ENVIRONMENT NEEDS TO BE RISK-INFORMED

Even though Romania has taken important steps to strengthen the legislative and organizational framework for disaster mitigation and preparedness, policies aimed at reducing private asset losses and increasing resilience could be further enhanced. Policies aimed at reducing private asset losses—including reducing the exposure and vulnerability of assets and improving access to early warning systems—could reduce asset losses by up to 13 percent and well-being losses by 16 percent (Hallegatte et al. 2017). Likewise, policies aimed at increasing resilience—including providing access to savings, insurance, and finance, and accelerating reconstruction through access to finance and streamlined processes, postdisaster support etc.—could reduce asset losses by 2.8 percent and well-being losses by 14 percent (Hallegatte et al. 2017).

Improving resilience to natural disasters will require enhanced cross-sectoral coordination and mainstreaming of climate change considerations in the design and implementation of resilience policies and measures. For instance, with climate in the Southeastern part of Romania—which is also the area with most arable lands and high-value farming—becoming semi-arid, the agro-climatic and economic conditions of agriculture are likely to be significantly modified. As the availability of water becomes an increasing constraint in the area, the improvement in irrigation systems will be critical for minimizing anticipated negative impacts, thereby highlighting the need for water and agricultural Programme for International Student Assessment policies to be closely coordinated. Moreover, to maximize the effects of sectoral policies and measures aimed at building resilience to natural disasters, climate change considerations should be considered in policy design and implementation. For instance, flood risk assessments developed as part of the EU Flood Directive were based on historical data from the past 35 years. Since the design parameters are expected to change in the future, given changing rainfall patterns, there is a need for the next generation of river flood risk assessments, flash flood, and drought assessments to properly account for climate change.

The availability of funding and investments to support effective climate policies and disaster risk reduction measures are limited. Even though Romania has complied with the requirements of the Floods Directive by submitting the FRMPs in 2016, under-funding has been persistent. For instance, considering current flood risks—and the climate change impacts that are expected to further exacerbate them—major investments will be needed to improve protection from downstream flooding and to increase storage to offset droughts. But water resource management in Romania has been regularly under-funded since the 1990s, with the Romanian Waters National Administration (ANAR) suffering from institutional and financial weaknesses, including insufficient revenues from bulk water tariffs that prevent it from being able to carry out proper maintenance of hydraulic assets (World Bank, 2017a).

Similarly, the lack of investment in seismic risk reduction in the building sector has also been an issue. In Bucharest alone, 2,563 residential blocks were identified as needing structural strengthening from vulnerability in the event of a future earthquake. Furthermore, there were an estimated 607 residential buildings in the Class I, the highest seismic risk category across the country. These buildings contained 10,577 dwelling units with serious structural deficiencies, most of which were occupied. More than 60 percent of those were located in Bucharest (World Bank, 2015). Moreover, many public buildings, including emergency response headquarters, fire and rescue stations, police stations, command centers, public administration buildings, and educational facilities have been assessed as being at high risk of partial or complete collapse during an earthquake. Therefore, there is a need to scale up the government's financing for retrofitting both the residential and public sector building stock, to minimize potential damage in the event of an earthquake, to increase residents' awareness of the urgency of addressing these risks, and to undertake measures to improve adequate transitional shelters to accommodate residents during the retrofitting period.

The coordination among various stakeholders involved in disaster preparedness and risk reduction needs to be improved, and their capacity enhanced. Today, the organizational set-up for disaster risk management in Romania comprises a system of institutions that include central and local public administrations. For instance, local authorities are required to have hazard and risk maps for their territorial administrative units, but these are reportedly incomplete, inconsistent, out of date, or simply not available for some cities. The extent to which these plans account for the full array of climate impacts anticipated across Romania is also unclear. Part of the challenge arises from how climate change is treated from a planning perspective—as purely an emergency response issue, or as something that can be planned for and adequately addressed over time through capital investment and policy changes (World Bank, 2014). For these reasons, there is a need to strengthen the capacity to design and implement risk reduction measures, and to facilitate access to sufficient funds.

NOTES

1. These included 44 floods, 15 extreme temperature events, 7 storms, 2 earthquakes, 1 drought, and 1 landslide. To be classified as a disaster, it must conform to at least one of the following criteria: 10 or more dead, 100 or more affected, declaration of a state of emergency or a call for international assistance (EM–DAT).
2. EM–DAT 1990–2017 (The Emergency Events Database—Université Catholique de Louvain—CRED, D. Guha-Sapir. www.emdat.be, Brussels, Belgium).
3. 2017 Escalating impact of climate extremes on critical infrastructure in Europe. Global Environmental Change.
4. GDP that is normalized (weighted) by inflation and population.
5. For the purpose of this report, resilience to natural disasters and climate change are defined as measures that are aimed at reducing sensitivity or at increasing adaptive capacity to natural disasters or longer-term climate change impacts.

6. Romania National Institute for Earth Physics Earthquake Catalogue.
7. Vulnerability to seismic risk is due to Romania's geographical location on the Vrancea subduction zone. Proximity to the fault and poor soils mean that Bucharest is among Europe's capital city with the highest disaster risk and one of the 10 most vulnerable cities to seismic risks in the world.
8. In 1978 values.
9. According to the World Bank Data (GDP in current US$).
10. GFDRR: www.thinkhazard.org
11. For example, according to climate predictions, a shortening by seven days of the vegetation period in maize is possible by 2020, and a twelve-day shortening by 2050 because of increasing air temperatures and 14 percent lower yields by 2020 and 21 percent lower yields by 2050, respectively, as a result of higher in-soil water deficits mainly during the grain fill period (July–August). See Romania's 6th Sixth National Communication on Climate Change and First Biennial Report to the United Nations Framework Convention on Climate Change (2013).
12. As of 2013, only 1.2 percent of the utilized agricultural area was irrigated in Romania, compared with 2.1 percent in Bulgaria, 3 percent in Hungary, over 5 percent in France and the Netherlands, and more than 20 percent in Cyprus, Italy, Macedonia, Greece, and Malta.

REFERENCES

Armaş, Iuliana, Dragos Toma-Danila, Radu Ionescu, and Alexandru Gavriş. 2017. "Vulnerability to Earthquake Hazard: Bucharest Case Study, Romania." *International Journal of Disaster Risks Science* 8 (2) 2: 182–95.

European Commission. 2017. *Atlas of the Human Planet 2017: Global Exposure to Natural Hazards*, by Pesaresi, Martino, Daniele Ehrlich, Thomas Kemper, et al. Policy Report. Luxembourg: OECD.

FAO (Food and Agricultural Organization of the United Nations). 2015. *The Impact of Disasters on Agriculture and Food Security*. Rome: FAO.

General Inspectorate for Emergency Situations. 2016. "Country report - 5.1 Conditionality - Romania 2016."

Hallegatte, Stephane, Adrien Vogt-Schilb, Mook Bangalore, and Julie Rozenberg. 2017. *Unbreakable: Building the Resilience of the Poor in the Face of Natural Disasters*. Climate Change and Development Series. Washington, DC: World Bank.

Pavel, Florin. 2016. "Next Future Large Earthquake in Romania: A Disaster Waiting to Happen?" *Seismological Research Letters*, 88 (1): 1–3.

Romania, Ministry of Environment and Climate Change. 2013. *Romania's Sixth National Communication and First Biennial Report to the United Nations Framework Convention on Climate Change (UNFCCC)*.

Văcăreanu, R., Aldea, A., Lungu, D., Pavel, F., Neagu, C., Arion, C., Demetriu, S., Iancovici, M. 2016. Probabilistic Seismic Hazard Assessment for Romania. In: D'Amico, S. (Eds) *Earthquakes and Their Impact on Society*, Springer Natural Hazards Book Series, p. 137-169.

World Bank. 1978. *Romania —Post Earthquake Construction Assistance Project*. Washington, DC: World Bank.

——. 2014. *Romania: Urban Sector Rapid Assessment*. Washington, DC: World Bank Group.

——. 2015. *Housing in Romania: Towards a National Housing Strategy*. Washington, DC: World Bank Group.

——. 2017a. *Romania Water Diagnostic*. Washington, DC: World Bank Group.

——. 2017b. *Disaster risk profiles – Romania*. Washington, DC: World Bank Group.

——. 2017c. *Europe and Central Asia - Country risk profiles for floods and earthquakes*. Washington, DC: World Bank Group.

——. 2018. Background Note for the Romania Systematic Country Diagnostic. Climate and Disaster Risk Management.

5 Strengthening Institutions for Inclusive Growth

DESPITE PROGRESS, GOVERNANCE REMAINS ROMANIA'S KEY BINDING CONSTRAINT

The governance elements of this SCD look into the underlying determinants of constraints to achieve inclusive growth, shared prosperity, poverty reduction, and resilience.[1] This chapter examines the ways in which underlying power asymmetries among key actors in the policy process and the administration of justice result in systemic corruption and functional breakdowns that undermine public sector effectiveness, private sector productivity, and citizen engagement. These aspects ultimately affect the quality of Romania's public services and business environment, as well as the public's trust in government. As shown in the previous chapters, governance challenges have led to insufficiently inclusive growth, insufficient use of EU resources, and poor long-term planning to improve resilience:

- Weak governance has created an uncertain business environment, misallocation of resources to state-owned enterprises and politically connected firms, and insufficient utilization of EU funds.[2]
- Unequal opportunities have prevailed because of weak commitment to policy implementation, weak local service delivery, and an inability to ensure sufficient local funding as a result of patronage-based politics, which has left behind large parts of the population.
- Resilience in the face of natural disasters and climate change is constrained by lack of coordination between central and local authorities.

This chapter focuses on the decade since Romania's EU accession, arguing that, despite progress, particularly in judicial anti-corruption work, the fundamental institutions necessary for inclusive growth remain stunted. The chapter concentrates on the period since EU accession, but the 1990–1999 initial postsocialist transition and the 1999–2008 EU accession process helped to shape Romania's governance performance over this period. In the 1990s, Romania undertook gradual market-oriented reforms. It experienced slow private sector development, as private enterprises faced a difficult institutional environment and could not compete with state firms benefitting from subsidies and tax bailouts (Phinnemore, 2006). The subsequent EU accession process led to substantial reforms as Romania consolidated multi-party democracy, reduced state control over the economy, and developed a number of regulatory and anti-corruption agencies. Most notably, the Romanian National Anti-Corruption Directorate (DNA) was created in 2002 to address medium and high-level corruption cases; the National Integrity Agency (ANI) was set up in 2007 to verify declarations of assets and interests to uncover unjustified wealth and conflicts of interest; and the General Anticorruption Directorate (GAD) in the Ministry of Interior began to make progress implementing prevention activities, training, and risk assessments in subordinate institutions.

In the past decade since EU accession, these institutions have successfully pursued high-level prosecutions and helped to disincentivize corruption by increasing the perceived likelihood and costs of being caught. In 2015 alone, DNA prosecuted more than 1000 cases, including a sitting Prime Minister, five ministers, 24 Parliamentarians, 112 leaders from municipalities and city councils, and 32 directors of national companies. Up to 90 percent of cases originated from citizens' complaints,[3] helping to build trust. In 2016, 60 percent of Romanians said they had confidence or great confidence in DNA, compared with less than 11 percent for Parliament (INSCOP Research, 2016).[4] Sanctions from ANI, together with the transparency component of the assets and interest —in 2016, ANI published almost 7 million asset declarations—have also reduced incentives for corruption. These anti-graft institutions have become models that other countries are studying and replicating in the region.[5]

Despite success in prosecuting several high-level corruption cases, Romania's approach to anti-corruption work has not sufficiently addressed underlying problems, and now faces backlash and diminishing returns, as evidenced by demonstrations over the past year. More work is needed on prevention, where progress has been piecemeal and identified with individuals rather than institutions.[6] Institutions focused on prevention remain the exception rather than the norm.[7] Moreover, the top-down approach may be reaching its limits. Administrative controls established by the ANI have led to no significant cases of unlawful profit from conflict of interest, and although asset recovery has become a government priority, the rate of recovery remains low, at about 10 percent. Since 2016, trust in the judiciary has declined, and hundreds of thousands of people have gone to the streets to protest political efforts perceived to weaken the judicial process and undermine anti-corruption efforts across all branches of government. The underlying challenge is that top-down efforts have not alleviated deeper systemic problems: corruption is not a "disease" that can be eliminated, but rather a consequence of deep-rooted systemic deficiencies in state behavior and state-society interactions.

More broadly, reforms stemming from the EU accession process have not resulted in the transformative governance improvements that many hoped for and expected. Frequently, *de jure* reforms were poorly implemented, as old institutions resisted change. According to the World Economic Forum's *Global Competitiveness Report*, Romania's institutional evolution has stagnated over the past decade, with gains only witnessed in terms of transparency. Romania continues to perform poorly in terms of government favoritism, wastefulness, and diversion of public funds. It has not managed consistent state reforms that will increase the capacity needed for better public service delivery and sustainable growth. This leads to a general perception of failure of the Romanian society to reward merit, which contributes to skilled labor migration on a perilous scale.

Further enhancing the investment climate is paramount to create a level playing field for the private sector. As discussed in Chapter 2, to increase private sector investment and enhance the efficiency of the economy, reforms are needed to facilitate SOE performance (including through privatizations), reduce the state footprint, establish more transparent systems and capable institutions, and increase predictability in the legislative and regulatory environment.

As an upper-middle-income economy looking to converge with the (high-income) EU average, Romania has no choice but to address its governance challenges, as only middle-income countries that resolve key governance challenges are able to converge with high-income countries (box 5.1). To generate inclusive

BOX 5.1

The "middle-income trap" and the need to reform accountability institutions

Many countries experience growth stagnation at middle-income levels, a so-called "middle-income trap." Although many analyses look at policy causes and

proximate economic reasons for this middle-income growth stagnation, an alternative approach argues that the middle-income trap can instead be explained

Figure B5.1.1

Romania is underperforming the upper-middle-income "escapees" in terms of corruption and impartiality of public administration

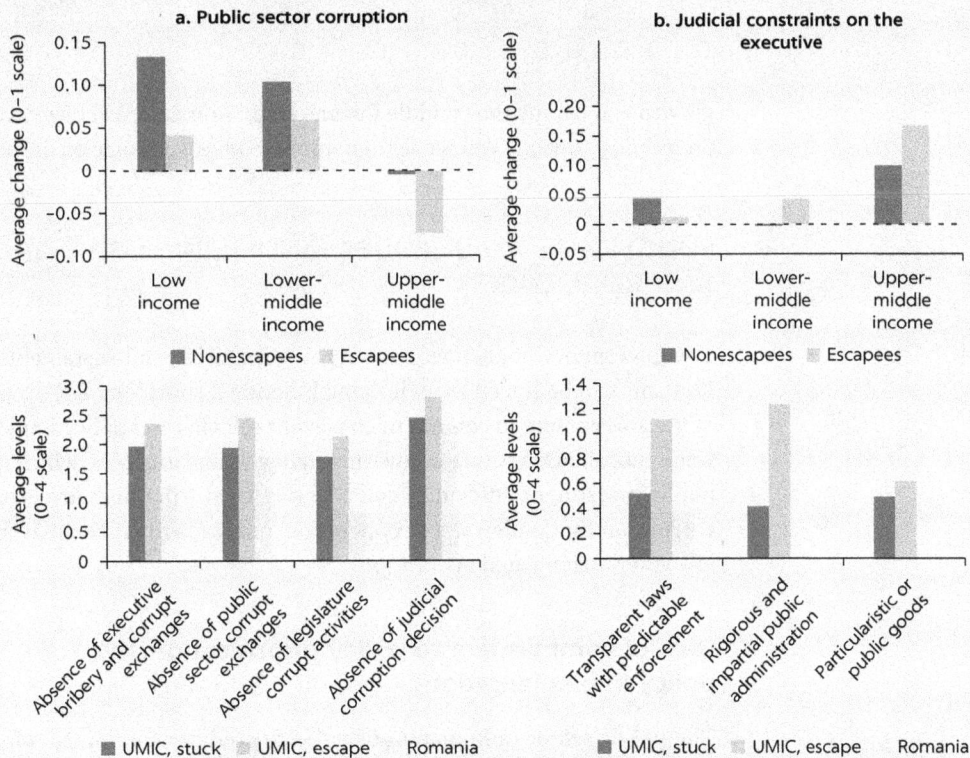

Sources: World Development Report 2017; V-Dem Dataset 7.1 from the Varieties of Democracy (V-Dem) Project (2017); World Bank calculations.
Note: In the top two figures, the bars represent average change on a scale of 0 to 1 in the relevant category for all "nonescapees" (dark blue) and "escapees" (light blue) during the time when a country is at the income level specified. The bottom two figures show average levels for each category on a scale of 0 to 4. UMIC = upper-middle income.

(continued)

BOX 5.1, *continued*

by power imbalances that prevent the institutional transitions necessary for productivity growth. Trapped middle-income economies are unable to adapt their growth models to sustain TFP growth by improving the efficient allocation of resources across sectors, and across firms within sectors, through processes of "creative destruction," or through processes of industrial upgrading. Both efficient resource allocation and industrial upgrading require new institutions whose creation may be blocked by vested interests that would lose out from creative destruction and competition.

Deals-based, often corrupt, interactions between firms and the state may actually help ensure commitment and coordination among state and business actors at low levels of income, but these deal-based relationships become problematic at higher income levels when they cannot substitute for impartial enforcement of contracts in more complex economies. Empirically, and consistent with this, upper-middle-income "escapees" lower their levels of corruption significantly before becoming high-income countries, while "nonescapees" see no improvement. Combatting corruption requires more accountable institutions, and indeed, the empirical evidence shows that legislative, judicial, media, and civil society checks improve more in countries that escape upper-middle-income status than those that do not escape. In this context, it is clear that Romania has a long way to go, clearly underperforming the upper-middle-income "escapees" in terms of corruption, transparency, policy implementation, and the impartiality of public administration, while appearing much more similar to the set of "nonescapees".

growth and escape the "middle income trap," Romania will have to confront its underlying power asymmetries and improve its governance environment.

FUNCTIONAL CHALLENGES HINDER INCLUSIVE GROWTH AND RESILIENCE

The governance challenges constraining inclusive and sustainable growth in Romania can be traced to underlying functional shortcomings: frequent failure of the government to commit to consistent reforms and policy implementation; weak coordination between government levels and agencies, which undermines public investment efficiency; and a lack of trust from high levels of perceived corruption that undermines cooperation and leads to citizen exit (brain drain, low voter turnout, and tax evasion).

Lack of commitment to policy prioritization and policy implementation

The public sector in Romania struggles to credibly commit to reforms and to policy implementation. Stop-and-go public policies and frequent changes in government highlight the lack of commitment, which, among other things, is apparent in pro-cyclical fiscal policies and the excessive use of emergency ordinances. Accountability and decision making are impeded by political instability—both within and across political parties—and the frequent turnover of officials. For example, from 2007 to 2017, Romania changed education ministers 17 times and finance ministers 14 times, and the past three years have seen five different prime ministers.

Weak commitment capacity creates a difficult environment for firms to make long-term investment decisions. Frequently changed legislation and regulations pose a difficulty for firm operations, with 82 percent of surveyed firms in Romania agreeing that fast-changing legislation and policies are a problem when doing business (European Commission, 2017). Credible commitment to property rights is necessary to provide market participants with the confidence to invest, but Romania leads the region in both lawsuits and violations in the area of property, with nearly ten thousand cases admitted by the European Court of Human rights (ECTHR).[8] Perceptions data suggest that the security of private contracts is lower than in any other EU country (figure 5.1).

Evidence of the government's challenge in committing to policies is apparent in the frequent use of "emergency ordinances," which are implemented before receiving Parliamentary approval. This procedure avoids consultations, and also leads to instability because when ordinances eventually reach Parliament they are frequently amended, even after already being partially implemented. Emergency ordinances were used 339 times in 2008 and 2009 under a minority and then a grand coalition government; fell to 117 in 2013 and 95 in 2014 under a coalition enjoying two thirds of Parliament seats; and rose to over 100 again in 2016 under a technocratic government.[9]

Given the strong possibility of reversal and amendment, the implementation of emergency ordinances is at times particularly poor. For example, given that half of total SOE debt in Romania is overdue and many SOEs are technically insolvent, with their survival based solely on periodic write-offs or debt-to-equity conversions (European Commission 2016). Government Emergency Ordinance 109/2011 (GEO 109/2011) sought to professionalize SOE boards and management. GEO 109/2011 was modified in 2016 under Law 111/2016. Despite evidence of better performance in SOEs that have implemented Law 111/2016 and its predecessor, GEO 109/2011, as of 2017 only 35 of the 147 SOEs obligated to apply it had actually finalized the selection procedures, while many have only interim boards. This situation results in continued politicization of some SOE

FIGURE 5.1

Security of private contracts is low

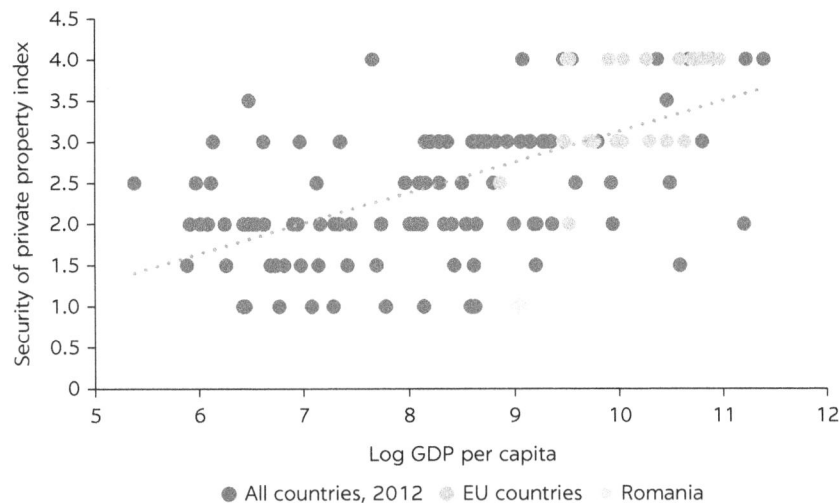

Sources: Institutional Profiles Database 2012; World Bank calculations.

FIGURE 5.2

Fiscal policy is procyclical

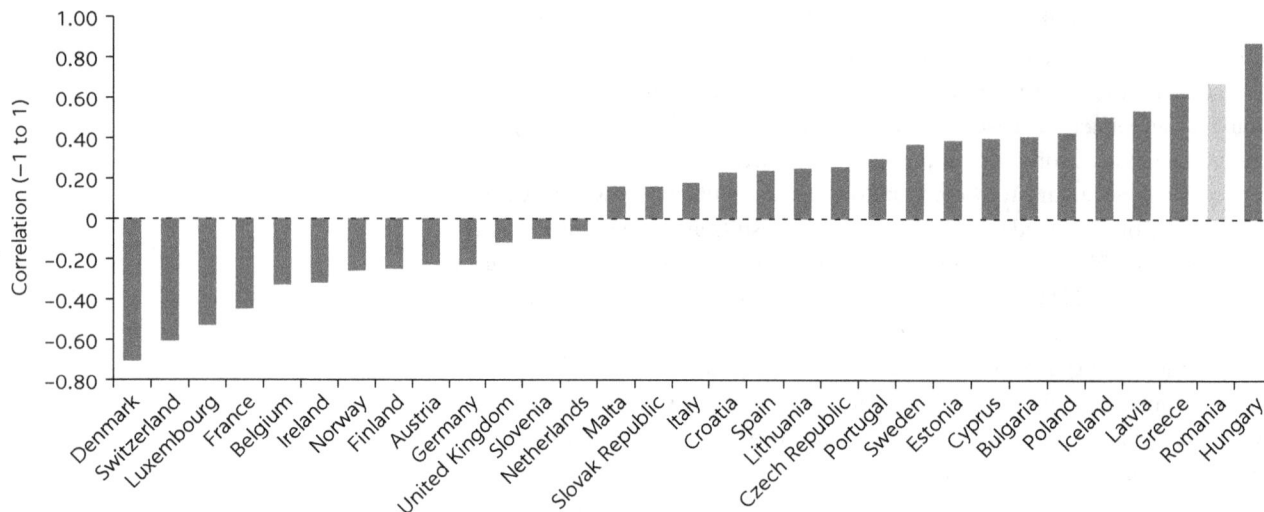

Sources: Eurostat and World Bank estimations.
Note: The cyclical components of the real government expenditure and real GDP have been estimated using the Hodrick-Prescott filter, on 1995–2016 data. Government expenditures have been deflated using the GDP deflator (see Vegh and Vuletin 2015).

boards and in the high turnover of board members—many appointed on an interim basis that undermines SOE strategic vision and independence. Moreover, the Parliament has diluted the provisions of Law 111/2016, including by exempting a large number of the most important SOEs from its application. These provisions, however, were rejected by the Constitutional Court in early 2018 for being unconstitutional.

In the fiscal realm, Romania struggles to commit to counter-cyclical fiscal policies (figure 5.2) and instead adopts frequent changes to fiscal legislation. Fiscal legislation is frequently amended regarding both fundamental issues, such as VAT or pension contributions, but also minor matters, creating significant challenges for firms' accountants and uncertainties for potential investors, while ultimately curtailing the ability of firms to make investment decisions, implement investments, hire, etc. Important bills lack real impact studies and are frequently issued on the basis of trial and error mechanisms, leading them to then be corrected while implementation is already underway. Figure 5.3 captures the changes across the years through various legislative means.

The weak commitment capacity to deliver on long-term objectives undermines the ability to generate long-term sectoral policies that improve service delivery in areas like education that could boost human capital and equality of opportunity. The first education law, passed in 1995, was changed 61 times until a new comprehensive education law (1/2011) was adopted.[10] The 2011 law was passed shortcutting debates in the Parliament, and amendments started immediately afterwards, increasing after a change in government. Six years later, the most ambitious provisions of the law, tying performance to budgets or assessing the performance of PhD schools,[11] have not been implemented, while there have been more than 100 changes to the law through emergency ordinances. Meanwhile, Romanian students are broadly one-and-a-half years of schooling behind students in EU countries.[12]

FIGURE 5.3

The fiscal code changes frequently

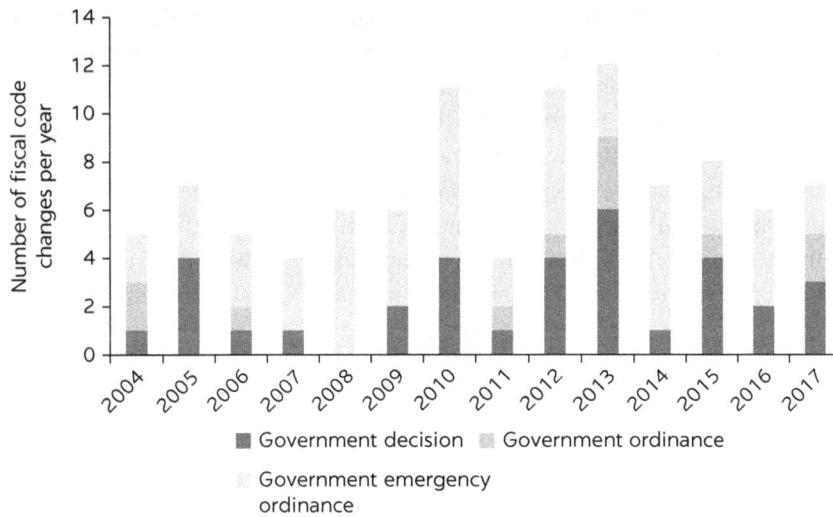

Source: Chamber of Deputies legislative portal.

Weak coordination between and among public administration units and businesses

Although Romania's public sector employs 25 percent of the total number of employees,[13] it underperforms in many areas and is often unable to deliver necessary public services at EU standards. Weak coordination between government levels and agencies undermines public sector efficiency, while weak coordination between state agencies and businesses undermines processes for industrial upgrading. Weak coordination is evidenced by low public investment efficiency, tax collection below expectations, and a low level of internal information, communication, and administrative control.

Fragmentation of sectoral responsibilities has led to diffuse accountability and poor intersectoral coordination. Public policy units in line ministries were designed and staffed during EU accession and soon after, and then insufficiently staffed and consolidated—for example in health and education— given a lack of commitment to connect strategic and budget planning to ministerial day-to-day operations. Instead, decision making remains concentrated at the political level, increasing the risk of ad hoc decisions, indicated by the high number of emergency ordinances and amendments to legislation discussed in the previous section. Laws and regulations are frequently introduced without proper interagency coordination and with limited policy substantiation based on weak analytical foundations (World Bank, 2017).

Poor access to information and weak transparency further limit the potential for accountability and improved coordination. For instance, according to Romania's Freedom of Information Act (Law 544/2001) all public authorities have to publish a yearly report accounting for all activities related to their mission and funds. Yet of a total of 1,484 annual reports from 2001 to 2017, only 449 were identified online and after legal requests, resulting in a rate of formal compliance of 30 percent, and only 227 of these annual reports contained all of the legally required information, resulting in a substantive compliance rate of just 15 percent.[14]

The most notable negative consequences of weak coordination in agencies and among levels of government are deep inefficiencies in public spending and bottlenecks in the absorption of EU funds. In 2015, for example, spending on public investment was 25 percent lower than planned, despite access to EU funds. Between 2007 and 2013, Romania received about EUR 15.4 billion from the European Regional Development Fund (ERDF) and the Cohesion Fund (CF), equivalent to 25.1 percent of government capital investment, but as of March 2018, Romania had absorbed only 17 percent of the EUR 30.9 billion of EU funds allocated for the 2014–2020 programming period. This situation is largely attributable to capacity constraints in project planning and implementation in the public sector. Historically, there has been little alignment of strategic priorities and budgetary commitments. Many ministries have strategic documents with no budget or funding sources identified; consequently, their strategic priorities are never supported through funded projects or programs.[15] Cost and time overruns are pervasive. Amendments made in 2016 to the GEO no. 88/2013 provide a budgeting mechanism for significant public investment projects, but the prioritization is not sufficiently linked to budgetary allocations, and there has been inflation of the project portfolio, as well as insufficient funding of ongoing projects. This helps explain why 93 percent of surveyed companies in Romania consider inadequate infrastructure to be a problem, far more than any other EU country, with Italy being next at 77 percent (European Commission, 2017 and figure 5.4).

The transportation sector is one of the main intended beneficiaries of EU funds, and showcases the underlying capacity constraints and lack of funding prioritization. The use of European Cohesion and Structural Funds available to the Romania's transport sector—about EUR 4.6 billion between 2007 and 2013—could have significantly boosted the funding of transport investments during a period of severe fiscal stress in Romania, but the Ministry of Transport (MOT)

FIGURE 5.4

Investment in infrastructure is high but the quality is low in Romania

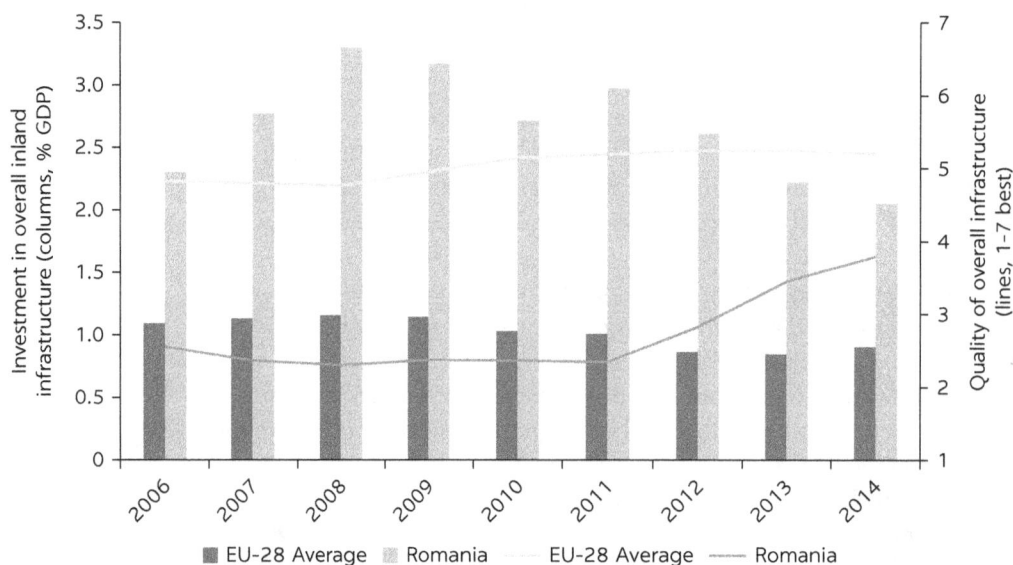

Source: Eurostat World Competitiveness Report, 2014–15.

and the implementing entities have been unable to utilize such grants because of poor sector governance and corporate governance, highlighted by weaknesses in administrative capacity and inadequate funding prioritization. Although the Fiscal Responsibility Law requires the MOT to prepare budget proposals consistent with its strategic goals and with the annual ceilings issued by the Ministry of Public Finance, requiring the MOT to develop strict prioritization mechanisms, there remains no clear link between the stated policy goals and the spending program. This inability to satisfactorily prioritize and manage projects has meant that funding of new projects has been spread too thinly, and a ballooning capital investment program has been overloaded with unfunded or inadequately funded projects. For instance, in 2010 the total authorized annual capital expenditure for all modes of transport was more than six times the MOT's total annual budget, and more than eight times the previous average annual capital expenditures (World Bank, 2010). As a consequence, Romania's road infrastructure costs remain extraordinarily high even compared to EU average, at a quality of road infrastructure very similar to Bulgaria's.

Coordination challenges underlie the absence of an effective national transport strategy that prioritizes objectives according to absorptive capacity and can guide both public and private participants in the industry. The MOT itself is modally and functionally fragmented into numerous directorates, and is tactical and reactive in its approach; political deliberations disproportionately shape its deliberations rather than technical considerations (World Bank, 2010). Moreover, there is an unclear division of roles between the MOT and the road and rail infrastructure companies, leading to insufficient distance between the regulatory watchdogs and the regulatory policy makers on the one hand, and the regulated parties on the other. The four transport entities[16] have not become autonomous state-owned companies responsive to their markets, but instead remain branches of the MOT reincarnated in corporate form. This has been inimical to the focused long-term planning and operational management necessary to deliver efficient transport infrastructure and services. As one consequence, train companies have been operating with an imbalance between their revenues and expected service levels; they now generate the most arrears among central and subnational SOEs. An example in this sense is CFR Marfa, which was the second-ranked SOE in terms of outstanding payments, as of 2016.

Corruption undermines trust and reduces the scope for cooperation

Corruption undermines trust in the state and state legitimacy. Trust in most public institutions remains low (figure 5.5), and these low levels of trust undermine cooperation, defined as voluntary compliance by citizens with state regulations and norms. Popular perceptions of corruption remain high (figure 5.5): 93 percent of Romanians think that corruption is widespread; 57 percent are personally affected by corruption; 25 percent report having been asked to give a bribe; and 28 percent report that additional payments are required for health services—the highest figure in Europe, compared to a 5 percent average (European Commission, 2014). Forty-six percent of Romanians believe that corruption has increased despite the anticorruption crackdown, 35 percent believe that it stayed the same, and only 18 percent see some improvement (Mungiu-Pippidi and Dadasov, 2016; IRES, 2017).

FIGURE 5.5

Trust is low and corruption is widespread

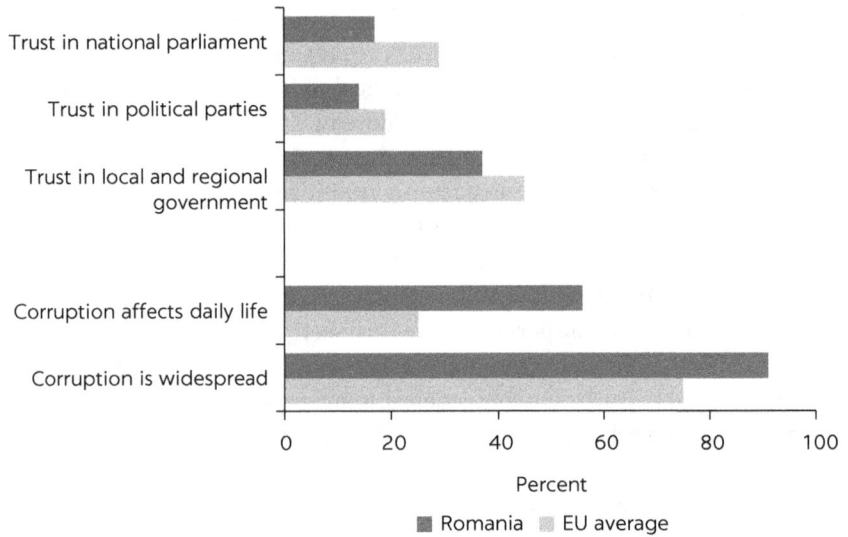

Source: European Research Centre for Anti-Corruption and State-Building (ERCAS) 2015.

FIGURE 5.6

Romania has the highest VAT gap in the EU

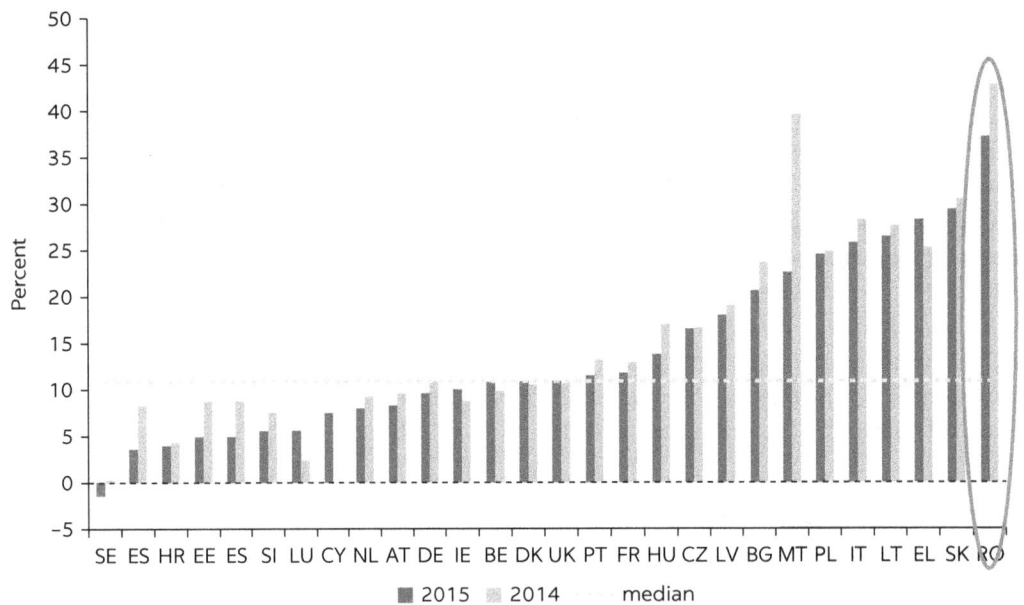

Source: TAXUD 2017.
Note: Value-added-tax (VAT) gap is the difference between what is collected and what should theoretically be collected, measuring enforcement and compliance.

A low level of trust breaks down cooperation, prevents citizens from playing a proactive role in ending the poor governance cycle, and leads to citizen exit—both literally, through migration, and figuratively, by not voting or not contributing to public goods provision, and by evading taxes. Despite growing among the fastest in Europe in the recent years, Romania, a country with eighteen million registered voters,[17] has only a little over five million people employed,[18] largely as a consequence of migration, which greatly strains its social security and pensions budgets. Turnout for parliamentary elections has declined from 86 percent in 1990 to 65 percent in 2000 to 39 percent in 2008 and 2016, indicating decreased citizen engagement.[19] Romania also has high levels of tax evasion—as indicated by the highest VAT gap in the EU (figure 5.6)—which undermines state capacity.

UNDERLYING POWER ASYMMETRIES CAUSE CORRUPTION AND POOR GOVERNANCE

Underlying power asymmetries among the different actors in the policy process drive Romania's governance challenges; this has specific manifestations: for example, capture by vested interests and pervasive clientelism and patronage in the civil service, which lead to the functional challenges described in the previous section. Reforms to date have not addressed the underlying causes and enablers of persistent and pervasive corruption. In a weak commitment environment, corruption itself has served as a deals-based method of commitment among powerful actors.

Capture by vested interests leads to resource misallocation and undermines innovation

Capture by political elites allied with appointed officials across the three branches of the state, and other groups interested in maintaining the status quo, prevents inclusive growth and increased resilience. Party selection processes often rely on small and elitist groups of business; cross-party demand for the resources of these groups empowers the business groups themselves and undermines programmatic and consistent party platforms. Capture by "status-quoists"—who stand to gain from stunted institutions of accountability and political fluidity—has limited inclusive growth, slowed or blocked the evolution of institutions, and slowed convergence.

The transformation to a growth model based on firm entry, competition, and innovation has been impeded by actors who have benefited from early growth—and who therefore have limited incentives to join coalitions for further reforms. Many postcommunist transition economies have experienced "partial reform equilibria" in which winners from early economic reforms block further liberalization that would dissipate their concentrated rents (Hellman, 1998). In Romania, 90 percent of firms consider corruption to be a problem in doing business; 93 percent agree that favoritism hampers business competition; 86 percent agree that connections are the easiest way to obtain certain public services; 93 percent agree that corruption is caused by too-close links between business and politics; and 70 percent agree that the only way to succeed in business is to have personal connections—a higher share than any other EU country (European Commission, 2017).

Capture leads to the wasteful spending and misallocation seen in public procurement. Romania has dedicated the highest allocation reported in the EU to total public spending on the construction of public works, but with low returns given capture and corruption. Eighty percent of firms perceive corruption in public procurement managed by national authorities—the highest in the EU—while 83 percent of firms perceive corruption in public procurement managed by regional or local authorities—also the highest in the EU.

Direct measures of favoritism in public construction also demonstrate the high share of particularistic allocations. Three specific indicators were monitored to measure particularism: single bidding, meaning that only one bid is submitted to a tender in a competitive market; political connection, meaning that the contract was allocated to a politically connected firm (interest disclosures of public officials to ANI and public donation registers to political parties are the

FIGURE 5.7

Particularistic public procurement contracts have decreased but remain high

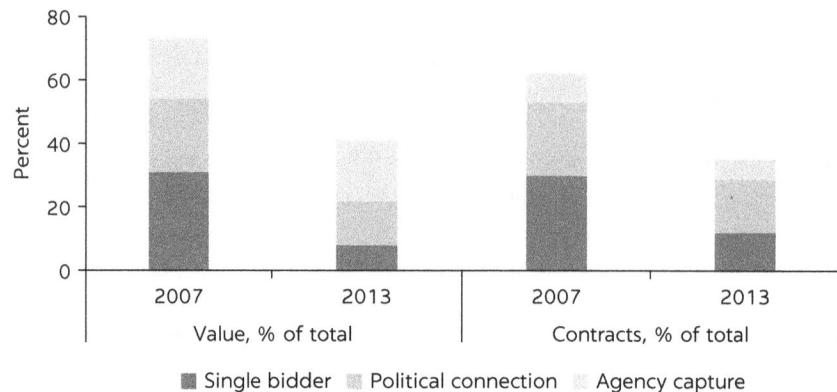

Source: Societatea Academică din România (SAR) (2015). Data based on official sources identifying construction sector contracts of more than 1 million euros awarded by public institutions.

sources for this data); and agency capture, meaning that a specific contracting agency grants more than 51 percent of its contracts or procurement budget to only one private contractor.[20] Figure 5.7 shows the share of particularistic allocations—52 percent in 2007, decreasing to 39 percent in 2013,[21] an improvement, but not as much of one as EU accession could have provided. Specifically, although the number of single-bidding contracts declined substantially, there was much less progress in terms of political connections and agency capture, which are more difficult to directly monitor.

Clientelism and patronage undermine public sector capacity

The public administration in Romania mirrors in many cases disputes in the political sphere, often acting as an extension of those tensions rather than as a public good working for citizens. Political patronage influences recruitment and placement of employees throughout the administration, and especially in key positions. As a consequence, the safety net provided by the existence of a professional bureaucracy sheltered from continuous political upheaval works only to some extent in Romania.

In the civil service, appointments to senior positions often depend on political patronage rather than merit. For example, a third of education ministers had problems with plagiarism disclosed in their own academic work. Patronage works its way down the system, reducing bureaucratic ability and creating norms that enable bribe-taking and preferential access to public services by front-line providers (figure 5.8).

Politicization has been achieved by a combination of restrictions of the Civil Service Authority (ANFP), derogations of procedures (for instance applications for permanent positions rather than temporary secondment), and open violations of legislation. For instance, in 2015, the last year when such a report was made public, the agency for civil servants approved 8,680 merit-based advancements not organized by itself, but by other authorities, compared with only 1,250 through its electronic portal that ensures objectivity—roughly a ratio of seven to one.[22]

The nonmeritocratic system leads to lack of trust, as discussed above, and undermines the innovation ecosystem. Science and research are marginalized

FIGURE 5.8
Special advantages in provision of public services, 2013

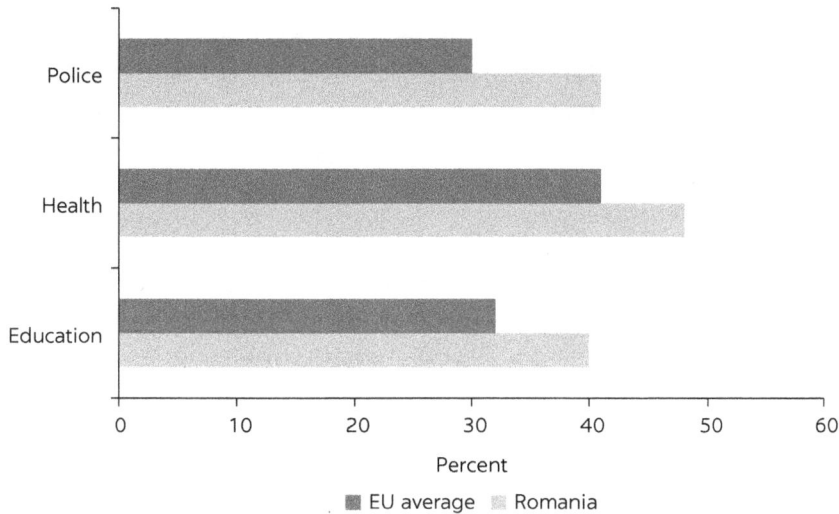

Source: ERCAS 2015.

because powerful actors choose not to invest in areas where returns are seen as too diffuse. As discussed in Chapter 2, the overall ecosystem for innovation is rated by the EU Innovation Scorecard as the second worst in Europe.[23] The government has an essential role to play in creating the infrastructure for merit and innovation, and in developing the benchmarks, but when numerous politicians make headlines for their own plagiarism, connections are further highlighted as the best channels to succeed in both public and private sectors.

Identifying reform priorities for more effective governance

Romania faces complex governance challenges that stunt inclusive growth and resilience. Boosting inclusive growth requires identifying appropriate incentives to catalyze the switch to a growth model based on firm entry, competition, and innovation. Inclusion requires service delivery to enhance human capital and job creation through the reform of labor market institutions. Resilience to natural disasters requires a risk-informed policy, legal, and institutional environment. This enables coordination among the central administration, local authorities, and other stakeholders involved in disaster preparedness and risk reduction, and requires a sustained commitment not to redirect disaster management funds for other purposes. These goals cannot be achieved without addressing underlying power asymmetries, as reforms are impeded by actors who benefited from early growth and may have limited incentives to join coalitions for further reforms.

Asymmetries in bargaining power by different actors can be addressed through actionable reforms, with achievable goals that demonstrate effectiveness and generate reform momentum. The priority areas for reform here involve rules that increase the political and legal cost of induced policy distortions related to transparency, a management framework for public investment, a reduction of the state's role in the economy, and in the more medium term, civil service reforms.

Increase transparency to enable collective action and enhance accountability

Greater transparency can help to reduce capture and clientelism, or at least to ameliorate the negative effects of these power asymmetries. Lack of transparency supports the status quo and weakens accountability. Trust in Romanian public institutions is at its lowest level since 1990; Romanian citizens do not trust that public institutions are working for them, and often believe false information. Technology and e-government were supposed to advance transparency, but Romania has one of the lowest scores in Europe, particularly in the "online service component."[24] According to the public integrity framework index, IPI, Romania performs poorly on freedom of the media (ranked 26th out of 30) and "enlightened" citizenry (ranked 30th out of 30). In other words, the grassroots collective action capacity to demand for good governance is weak; greater transparency can enhance this collective action capacity.

An important step would be improving the internal information and communication within various branches and tiers of government by more e-government, as well as the enforcement of current legislation to enhance public oversight. According to Romania's Freedom of Information Act (Law 544/2001), all public authorities have to publish a yearly report accounting for their activities according to their mission and funds, but compliance is very low, as discussed above. Additionally, in 2015 a portal hosted by the Ministry of Finance started to track expenses of all public authorities. The portal was eventually made public in 2016, but there is no compliance rate published or tracked, and there are no sanctions for noncompliance to help increase coverage. The low degree of information about what the government does, particularly at lower tiers, limits implementation capacity and oversight.

Develop a management framework for public investment for both budgetary and EU funds

Improving public spending efficiency is essential for Romania to achieve adequate public-sector outcomes at a reasonable cost. Poor governance leads to an ineffective use of funds. Historically, there has been little alignment of strategic priorities and budgetary commitments. Many ministries have numerous strategic documents with no budget or funding sources identified; and therefore, there are strategic priorities that are never supported through funded projects or programs. By March 2017, which officially marked the end of the 2007–2013 programming period, Romania was still struggling to spend its funds from the previous programming cycle[25] and was the EU country which lost the most EU funds because of poor administrative capacity and errors in the (re)allocation of funds, by setting unrealistic targets and estimates.[26] More than halfway into the 2014–2020 programming period, Romania is still stuck in the "absorption" problem—how much money is advanced and how much is actually reimbursed by the EU as having been spent correctly—with not enough attention given to the actual quality and "on the ground" impact of financed projects.

Public investment efficiency can be improved with a predictable fiscal policy framework and changes to the allocation of resources from the line ministries. Aligning annual budgets with strategic frameworks could help to reduce the scope for ad hoc policy decisions, contributing to more efficient government spending.[27] Also, the links between prioritization and budgetary allocations are weak, and the multi-year budget framework has been ineffective in preventing an inflation of the project portfolio and the insufficient funding of ongoing projects. The management framework for significant public investments with the National Program for Local Development (PNDL) and EU-funded investments can be integrated. Developing a management framework for public investment would need to take place across parties to ensure commitment. The creation of a unitary framework for public investment for five years, with both budgetary and EU funds, would be the end of ad hoc and clientelistic spending, and thus vested interests would be strongly opposed.

Reduce interactions with the state to shift towards anticorruption based on prevention

Anticorruption efforts need to shift toward prevention and away from a focus on prosecution, in particular by reforming control and audit institutions, and cutting red tape, bottlenecks, and privileged status for selected SOEs. Romania has more bureaucratic requirements than most EU countries, making the citizen and firm interaction with public institutions difficult and costly. Reducing interfaces with the state, and the number of administrative approvals necessary for firm operations and frontline service delivery, can help prevent corruption and increase trust in the state.

In addition to streamlining the role of the state, technology can also help to reduce potentially corrupt face-to-face interactions. For instance, the inadequate and uncoordinated digital framework of public institutions results in public offices seeking information from citizens that they should be able to procure from other public institutions directly. Romania could institutionalize digital coordination by concentrating on the most inefficient bureaucratic procedures and streamlining and digitizing them. This could include, in particular, simplifying online tax payments by citizens and businesses. Despite a few initiatives towards e-governance, Romania remains a paper-based society, and in many cases, for documents to be considered legally binding, there must be an original paper copy. A deeper review of the legal, procedural, and institutional arrangements and constraints to e-governance would be beneficial.

Reform the civil service

Romania needs deep public administration reforms, which will involve a longer-term process to depoliticize the public administration and create a professional senior management that reduces the bottlenecks of decision-making. Politicization of the public administration prevents professionalization and results in high turnover. A cross-party commitment to competitively recruit civil servants for nonpolitical positions to manage policy, operations, and service delivery may prove useful. These recruits could be permanent employees who serve across changes in political leadership.

This process can build on successful reform pilots previously undertaken by several agencies, including the implementation of modern IT systems, personnel evaluation systems, and enhanced monitoring. Certain agencies, such as the Competition Council, are already pursuing these reforms, but a system-wide approach could achieve great results. Romania could also seek to make civil servant positions more attractive for well-educated Romanians. The civil service is plagued by low salaries, limited career advancement and mobility, obsolete systems, resistance to change, and uncertainty. There is no official program to support the preparation of young professionals interested in a career in public service. As a result, the civil service skews old, with less than one-third under the age of 40, and fewer than 4 percent under 30.[28]

NOTES

1. *Governance* here refers to the process through which state and nonstate actors interact to design and implement policies within a given set of formal and informal rules that shape and are shaped by power. See World Bank (2017).
2. Four years into the 2014–2020 cycle, the utilization of EU funds lags at 4.9 percent at end-January 2018 (excluding the National Program for Rural Development).
3. European Commission, Technical report on Progress in Romania under the Co-operation and Verification Mechanism.
4. One may argue that confidence in DNA sharply dropped subsequently, due to uncovering of abuses made by branches of the institution.
5. General Anti-Corruption Directorate. http://www.mai-dga.ro/eng/about-us/mission
6. An Evaluation of the Impact of the National Anti-Corruption Strategy 2012–2015 in Romania, carried out by a group of independent experts, 19th May 2016.
7. Romania's latest National Anti-Corruption Strategy 2016–2020 has now shifted the dialogue toward prevention, and included a bottom-up approach that mandates each government institution to create and implement its own anti-corruption action plan, but the efficacy of this plan remains to be seen.
8. Mungiu-Pippidi and Stefan (2012). Romania also has the largest number of applications related to property pending before the ECTHR and still has an outstanding settlement to make due to systematic infringement of property rights towards ECTHR, which is paid in yearly installments by the Ministry of Finance and contributes towards the ESA budget deficit. See http://cursdeguvernare.ro/cifrele-primei-rectificari-bugetare-pe-2015-urca-deficitul-la-186-din-pib.html
9. "Ordonanțe de urgență emise în anul 2016 de catre Guvern" (Emergency Ordinances issued by the government in 2016), Chamber of Deputies website, http://www.cdep.ro/pls/legis/legis_pck.lista_anuala?an=2016&emi=3&tip=18&rep=0
10. http://www.gandul.info/stiri/fiecare-ministru-cu-legea-lui-cate-schimbari-a-suferit-sistemul-de-invatamant-in-ultimii-25-de-ani-13731545
11. http://sar.org.ro/wp-content/uploads/2016/11/Raport-CUC_traducere.pdf
12. According to the OECD, a 30-point score difference in PISA 2015 is equivalent to one year of schooling.
13. This figure covers public administration, education, health and social assistance, armed forces and assimilated personnel (MApN, SRI, MAI, etc.). National Institute of Statistics. It excludes employment in SOEs.
14. Romanian Academic Society, see http://www.romaniacurata.ro/buna-guvernare-pe-amb ele-maluri-ale-prutului-doar-30-din-institutiile-din-romania-si-99-din-r-mol dova-au-elaborat-vreodata-rapoarte-de-activitate/
15. The government has tried to address this issue at a national level, and is using the World Bank Strategy Unit RAS to improve coordination across government levels and sectors, and the Strategic Planning RAS to align strategic programs and budget.
16. The Romania National Company for Motorways and National Roads (RNCMNR), the National Railway (Infrastructure) Company (CFR SA), the National Railway (Passenger) Company (CFR Călători), and the National Railway (Freight) Company (CFR Marfa).
17. According to the Permanent Electoral Authority, based on the total number of Romanian voters registered in the Electoral Register, http://www.roaep.ro/
18. Excluding self-employment in agriculture.
19. Public Policies Institute, Bucharest.
20. For the methodology, see Mungiu-Pippidi, A. (2015); Doroftei, I. M. (2016).
21. Note that some procurement contracts are afflicted by multiple types of particularism, so the overall share of particularistic contracts is not the sum of the three sub-types.

22. http://www.anfp.gov.ro/R/Doc/2016/Raport%20activitate%20ANFP%202015/Raport
   _de_activitate_2015_FINAL.pdf, table 5
23. https://www.rvo.nl/sites/default/files/2017/06/European_Innovation_Scoreboard
   _2017.pdf
24. http://workspace.unpan.org/sites/Internet/Documents/UNPAN97453.pdf
25. http://www.fonduri-ue.ro/images/files/implementare-absorbtie/Anexa_1-Stadiul
   _absorbtiei_2007_-_2013_martie_2017.pdf
26. Notes from the Third Monitoring Committee on the Grand Infrastructure Operational
   Program 2014–2020, June 3, 2016, available at http://www.fonduri-ue.ro/poim-2014
   #implementare-ghiduri-beneficiari
27. Recently, the Government has worked to enhance the efficiency of public spending by
   linking the budgeting process to the strategic decision-making process. Through this ini-
   tiative, the Government has drafted and piloted a new methodology for developing and
   monitoring institutional strategic plans, seeking to ensure strategic priorities are funded
   through budgetary programs (Strategic Planning RAS). However, these reforms are still at
   early stages.
28. Data according to the 2015 Report on public employee's management and civil servants.

REFERENCES

Doroftei, Irina Madalina. 2016. "Measuring Government Favouritism Objectively: The Case of
   Romanian Public Construction Sector." *European Journal on Criminal Policy and Research*
   22 (3): 399–413.

ERCAS (European Research Centre for Anti-Corruption and State-Building). 2015. *Public
   Integrity and Trust in Europe.* Hertie School of Governance. Accessible at https://dsc.kprm
   .gov.pl/sites/default/files/pliki/public_integrity_and_trust_in_europe.pdf

European Commission. 2014. *Special Eurobarometer 397: Corruption.* Luxembourg: OECD.

———. 2016. "State-Owned Enterprises in the EU: Lessons Learnt and Ways Forward in a Post-
   Crisis Context." European Economy Institutional Paper No. 31, July 2016. Luxembourg:
   OECD.

———. 2017. *Flash Eurobarometer 457: Businesses' Attitudes Towards Corruption in the EU.*
   Luxembourg: OECD.

Hellman J. 1998. "Winners Take All: The Politics of Partial Reform in Postcommunist
   Transitions." *World Politics* 50 (2): 203-34.

INSCOP Research. 2016. *"Truth about Romania" Barometer* [Barometrul Adevărul despre
   România"].

IRES (Institutul Român pentru Evaluare și Strategie). 2017. "Percepții privind corupția în
   România – Raport de cercetare." [Perceptions regarding corruption in Romania Research
   Report], Unpublished opinion poll organized during 2–4 February 2017.

Mungiu-Pippidi, A., ed. 2015. *Government Favouritism in Europe. The ANTICORRP Project:
   Anticorruption Report*, Volume 3. Barbara Budrich Publishers.

Mungiu-Pippidi, Alina, and Ramin Dadasov. 2016. "Measuring Control of Corruption by a
   New Index of Public Integrity." *European Journal on Criminal Policy and Research* 22 (3),
   415–38.

Mungiu-Pippidi, A. and L. Stefan. 2012. "Perpetual Transitions: Contentious Property and
   Europeanization in South-Eastern Europe." *East European Politics and Societies* 26 (2):
   340–61.

Phinnemore, David, ed. 2006. *The EU and Romania: Great Expectations.* London: The Federal
   Trust for Education and Research.

SAR. 2015. "Romanian Public Procurement in the Construction Sector: Corruption Risks and
   Particularistic Links." Accessible at http://anticorrp.eu/wp-content/uploads/2015/06
   /D8.1.5-Romania.pdf.

TAXUD. 2017. *Study and Reports on the VAT Gap in the EU-28 Member States.* Warsaw: Institute for Advanced Studies. Accessible here: https://ec.europa.eu/taxation_customs/sites/taxation/files/study_and_reports_on_the_vat_gap_2017.pdf.

Vegh and Vuletin. 2015. "How is Tax Policy Conducted over the Business Cycle?" *American Economic Journal: Economic Policy* 7 (3).

World Bank. 2010. *Romania - Functional review: transport sector.* Washington, DC: World Bank.

——. 2017. *World Development Report on Governance and the Law.* Washington, DC: The World Bank.

6 Setting priorities for sustainable and inclusive growth

IDENTIFICATION OF PRIORITIES

Romania achieved an impressive reduction in poverty in the years leading up to the financial crisis, but progress has been slow since then, and a substantial welfare gap remains between the two Romanias. The past three decades in Romania have seen the consolidation of democratic institutions and an unprecedented increase in income per capita. The most dynamic firms and individuals have fully benefited from being part of the EU, with Bucharest and a handful of secondary cities becoming vibrant urban centers with growing populations and incomes. Yet vast segments of the population have been left behind and are unable to take advantage of opportunities.

Institutional challenges that are holding up structural reforms need to be addressed to unlock sustainable and inclusive growth. Weak commitment to policy implementation and influential vested interests help create an unfavorable business environment, holding back productive investment, both public and private, stunting innovation, and causing misallocation of resources. Lack of planning and poor horizontal and vertical coordination within government lead to weak local service delivery, constraining equal opportunities for the bottom 40. Finally, resilience to natural disasters and climate change, to which Romania is particularly exposed, is constrained by lack of coordination between central and local authorities.

The key lesson from this diagnostic is that, despite impressive economic growth, achieving shared prosperity and sustainable welfare improvements will remain a distant reality if Romania does not address its governance challenges. The identification of governance failures as the most binding development constraint sheds light on why economic growth continues to be volatile and noninclusive. Concerted efforts are needed to enhance commitment to long-term policy goals, while future policies need to acknowledge and target the underlying institutional challenges. Resolving these will be a long and difficult process, but the potential rewards will be high. This would also help Romania counter the consequences of a shrinking and aging population, and allow those at the bottom to contribute more actively to economic growth—which could trigger a virtuous cycle of inclusive growth and development.

Following the diagnostic in previous chapters and extensive consultations with various stakeholders, this SCD proposes a number of development priorities for Romania that will help enhance equity and shared prosperity. The list of priorities is very long, as difficult challenges remain in many key areas. Priorities are assessed based on two criteria: (i) their potential impact on reducing poverty and boosting shared prosperity; and (ii) how critical they are to addressing the constraints that keep Romania from advancing toward its goals. The reforms that address the most binding constraints—and represent higher order priorities in terms of their relevance—are noted as being highly critical. Also, priorities receive higher ratings if they are important for the sequencing of reforms and for helping to resolve other constraints. While not a consideration for the prioritization itself, the time horizon for the impact to materialize is also indicated in the last column.

Based on these criteria, four broad areas of priorities are identified: (i) increasing the effectiveness and efficiency of the state in public service delivery; (ii) catalyzing private sector growth and competitiveness; (iii) ensuring equal opportunities for all; and (iv) building resilience for sustainable growth. These priorities will inform the World Bank Group's engagement in Romania for the period 2019–2023. A detailed list of priorities is shown in table 6.1.

The governance priorities are considered as prerequisites, whereas the other three areas proposed are intended to be complementary and mutually supportive. For example, promoting human capital development will not only promote inclusion, but also enhance the overall skill composition of the labor force, thus contributing positively to growth. The three priority areas are supported by a fundamental pillar on governance reforms aimed at improving commitment to policy goals, as well as policy coordination and implementation.

KNOWLEDGE GAPS

We conclude this report with a list of key knowledge gaps that were discovered during the diagnostic. Filling these gaps would help policy makers assess the impact of policies and design more effective interventions. In what follows we include a list of topics where further research is needed to properly guide policymaking. We also indicate data gaps when relevant:

- Productivity analysis based on firm-level data. Use of panel data from a firm census or a structural business survey would allow to identify the impact of firm-level characteristics and market conditions on productivity growth. This would lead to a more nuanced understanding of the drivers of Romania's economic growth and of its pitfalls.
- Obstacles to female labor force participation. A deeper investigation into the impact of labor market and family policies on female labor force participation would help identify the biggest obstacles and priority intervention areas and groups.
- The broader welfare impact of emigration. Available surveys do not sufficiently capture patterns of intra-EU population movements and collect limited information on income from overseas employment or remittances. More data is needed to assess the welfare consequences of

high emigration on children left behind and to provide effective policy responses.

- Drivers of low geographic mobility. A systematic study is needed to explore the drivers behind the extremely low geographic mobility and how they can be addressed.
- The drivers and consequences of informality. Two household surveys are available within the last decade which allow some measurement of informal employment: the 2008 round of the European Social Survey and the 2016 round of the Life in Transition Survey. A detailed investigation of informality is difficult with these surveys, because of the limited information included and the small sample sizes. Better data would help understand the institutional factors and the drivers behind informality, from the firm and household side.
- The impact of labor market institutions on labor market outcomes. A better understanding is needed on how labor market institutions, notably minimum wage policies and employment protection legislation may impede the dynamism of the labor market and affect labor market outcomes (including the incidence of informality) of different population segments.

TABLE 6.1 **Matrix of priorities**

PRIORITY	EXPECTED IMPACT	CRITICALITY	TIME HORIZON
Increasing the effectiveness and efficiency of the state in public service delivery			
Increase transparency and access to information to enable collective action and enhance accountability.	Increase trust in institutions and cooperation of citizens to contribute to the financing of the provision of public goods	High	Medium term
Develop a management framework for public investment for budgetary and EU funds.	Improve efficiency of public spending, provide adequate supply of infrastructure and public services across the country	High	Short term
Reform the civil service aiming to depoliticize the public administration.	Increase efficiency and productivity of the public administration	High	Medium term
Catalyzing private sector growth and competitiveness			
Enhance infrastructure and connectivity by increasing investment in large transport infrastructure, including by mobilizing private financing instruments and expanding the use of public-private partnerships when sensible.	Increase productivity, support job creation and economic growth	High	Medium term
Create a vibrant business environment by cutting red tape, increasing the predictability of regulation, reducing the role of SOEs, reducing regulation of product markets, securing land titles and property rights, developing sustainable agribusiness and relevant value chains, strengthening financial intermediation and access to finance for MSMEs, and maintaining prudent economic policy management.	Reduce resource misallocations and support productivity and economic growth	Medium High	Short to medium term
Reduce labor market shortages, mismatches, and rigidities by increasing labor force participation, especially among women and the Roma, enhancing internal mobility for better allocation of labor and improving the minimum wage setting mechanism.	Increase labor force participation, labor productivity, and economic growth	Medium High	Short to medium term

continued

TABLE 6.1, *continued*

PRIORITY	EXPECTED IMPACT	CRITICALITY	TIME HORIZON
Ensuring equal opportunities for all			
Promote human capital development by investing in early childhood education and closing the gap in early school leaving, promoting vocational education and training (VET), achieving higher attainment in tertiary education and fostering lifelong learning; improving health outcomes and resolving inequities in access to high-quality health care through expanding primary care.	Support inclusive growth	High	Medium term
Achieve equitable access to high-quality public services by improving access to municipal infrastructure and delivering a robust social safety net that provides effective social assistance and integrated social services for the poor and marginalized groups, yet preserves work incentives.	Support inclusion	High	Medium term
Building resilience for sustainable growth			
Make the policy, legal and institutional environment risk-informed by enhancing readiness, reforming policies, and strengthening institutions for better disaster preparedness.	Reduce the physical, social and financial impact of disasters	Medium High	Medium term
Strengthen adaptation to climate change by enhancing and implementing cross-sectoral adaptation policies, measures, and financing options.	Reduce climate change vulnerabilities	Medium High	Medium term

Appendix
Key macro-fiscal and poverty indicators

	2005	2006	2007	2008	2009	2010	2011	2012	2013	2014	2015	2016	2017
Real GDP growth	4.2	8.1	6.9	8.5	−7.1	−0.8	1.1	0.6	3.5	3.1	3.9	4.8	6.9
Private consumption	9.6	11.6	12.1	7.2	−9.1	1.0	1.1	1.7	−2.4	4.4	5.5	7.3	9.0
Government consumption	2.1	−13	4.7	5.7	9.9	−12.3	−2.7	−5.6	23.7	0.5	−0.7	3.3	2.8
Gross fixed investment	15	20.6	50.5	17.6	−36.6	−2.4	2.9	0.1	−5.4	3.2	8.3	−3.3	4.7
Exports, goods and services	7.6	10.4	7.8	−3.2	−5.3	15.2	11.9	1.0	19.7	8	5.4	8.3	9.7
Imports, goods and services	16	22.6	28.8	0.2	−20.7	12.6	10.2	−1.8	8.8	8.7	9.2	9.8	11.3
Inflation (CPI, avg.)	9	6.6	4.8	7.8	5.6	6.1	5.8	3.3	4.0	1.1	−0.6	−1.5	1.3
Current account balance (% GDP)	−8.6	−10.4	−13.5	−11.3	−4.1	−4.4	−4.5	−4.4	−0.8	−0.5	−1.2	−2.1	−3.4
Financial and capital account (% GDP)	8.2	9.7	14.1	12.7	4.4	3.9	3.6	3.8	0.7	0.4	1.4	2.7	3.5
Net foreign direct investment (% GDP)	6.2	9.2	5.8	6.7	2.9	1.8	1.4	1.6	1.9	1.6	2.2	2.7	2.4
Fiscal balance (% GDP)	−0.7	−1.6	−2.3	−4.7	−7.1	−6.3	−4.2	−2.5	−2.5	−1.7	−1.3	−2.4	−2.8
General government debt, ESA (% GDP)	15.7	12.3	11.9	12.4	22.1	29.7	34.0	36.9	37.5	39.1	37.7	37.4	35.0
Primary balance (% GDP)	0.5	−0.9	−1.6	−4.0	−5.9	−4.9	−2.7	−0.7	−0.8	−0.2	−0.1	−1.1	−1.6
Poverty rate ($5.50/day 2011 purchasing power parity)	—	40.2	33.7	26.9	25.6	27.9	31.6	31.5	31.4	28.6	26.1	25.0	23.6
Gini of disposable income	—	0.38	0.36	0.34	0.34	0.33	0.34	0.34	0.35	0.34	0.34	—	—
Life expectancy at birth, total (years)	71.9	72.2	72.6	72.6	73.3	73.5	74.4	74.4	75.1	75.0	75.0	75.0	—

(continued)

	2005	2006	2007	2008	2009	2010	2011	2012	2013	2014	2015	2016	2017
Mortality rate, infant (per 1,000 live births)	15.1	13.7	12.3	11.1	10.2	9.7	9.3	8.9	8.5	8.1	7.8	7.7	—
School enrollment, primary (% net)	93.9	92.5	92.2	88.4	89.1	89.1	88.8	87.5	—	—	87.5	86.6	—
Population (millions)	21.3	21.2	20.9	20.5	20.4	20.2	20.1	20.1	20.0	19.9	19.8	19.7	19.6
Nominal GDP (US$ billions)	99.7	123.5	171.5	208.2	167.4	168	185.4	171.7	191.5	199.5	177.5	186.7	196.1
GDP per Capita (US$)	6,825	7,418	8,046	8,873	8,315	8,297	8,426	8,518	8,852	9,159	9,564	10,094	10,814

Source: World Bank, National Institute of Statistics, National Bank of Romania.
Note: Poverty and Gini figures pertain to income year. Gini is based on per capita income. — = not available.

www.ingramcontent.com/pod-product-compliance
Lightning Source LLC
Chambersburg PA
CBHW080427270326
41929CB00018B/3191